CW01506927

The printers

A collection of some 2500 technical terms, phrases, abbreviations and other expressions mostly relating to letterpress printing, many of which have been in use since the time of Caxton

Charles Thomas Jacobi

Alpha Editions

This edition published in 2019

ISBN : 9789353921835

Design and Setting By
Alpha Editions
email - alphaedis@gmail.com

As per information held with us this book is in Public Domain.
This book is a reproduction of an important historical work.
Alpha Editions uses the best technology to reproduce historical
work in the same manner it was first published to preserve its
original nature. Any marks or number seen are left intentionally
to preserve its true form.

THE

Printers' Vocabulary

A COLLECTION OF SOME 2500

TECHNICAL TERMS, PHRASES, ABBREVIATIONS

AND OTHER EXPRESSIONS

MOSTLY RELATING TO

Letterpress Printing

MANY OF WHICH HAVE BEEN IN USE SINCE THE
TIME OF CAXTON

By CHARLES THOMAS JACOBI

COMPILER OF " THE PRINTERS' HANDBOOK, ETC."

LONDON

THE CHISWICK PRESS, 21, TOOKS COURT

CHANCERY LANE

1888

INTRODUCTION.

Y little volume of last year, "THE PRINTERS' HANDBOOK OF TRADE RECIPES, ETC.," having met with a greater success than I had anticipated, I venture to offer the accompanying work as a small addition to our literature on Printing, trusting that it may be found useful for reference purposes, and especially so to those workers who are desirous of becoming acquainted with the terms, phrases, etc., used in the departments other than those they are employed in—the increasing tendency nowadays to subdivision of labour making it a somewhat difficult matter to acquire the expressions of the other branches of the trade. It may also be of service to publishers, authors, and others connected directly or indirectly with our craft, in making more clear the detail necessary between customer and tradesman.

I trust due allowance will be made for any possible difference of opinion in expressing the many brief definitions here attempted—circumstances and locality sometimes allowing of a slightly different construction—though, in the main, the same explanation.

The feature I have introduced in distinguishing those terms and phrases in use some two hundred years ago— a date equidistant with the invention of the art and the present time—may prove interesting, as many of them undoubtedly came into existence with the development of printing in this country by William Caxton and his successors four centuries since.

CHARLES THOMAS JACOBI.

November, 1888.

NOTE.

All the Terms and Phrases indicated by an asterisk are to be found in Joseph Moxon's " Mechanick Exercises," Vol. II., 1683.

THE PRINTERS' VOCABULARY

OF TECHNICAL TERMS, PHRASES, ABBREVIATIONS, AND OTHER EXPRESSIONS.

A

Is the signature used by the printer for the preliminary matter of a work.

ABBREVIATIONS.*—Characters or signs which indicate words or letters that have been shortened—such as record sorts in old books or reprints.

*Accents.—This term refers to the various signs used as accents which are cast singly for use with kerned letters.

*Accented letters.—Letters with various marks on used in our own and foreign languages for pronunciation or abbreviation, such as à é î ö ñ ā ĕ etc.

Accessories.—The tools and other small details necessary for the working of any press or machine.

Account books.—The class of books used in the commercial world for the keeping of accounts, such as ledgers, etc.

B

Account line.—Compositors working in companionships usually charge something " on account "—a vague item which is supposed to cover work in hand but not finished.

Account mark.—A sign thus $^a/_c$ used in commercial matters, meaning literally " account current."

*****Acute accent.**—A mark placed over a letter, thus á

Adams' machine.—An American platen machine, first invented by a person of the name of Adams some sixty years since.

Addenda.—The Latin plural for addition—appendices or something added to a book.

Addendum.—The Latin singular for " Addenda," which see.

Address cards.—Personal cards containing the name and address.

Admiration.—A punctuation mark, note of exclamation !

Admir.—Abbreviation used in the reading-room for "note of admiration."

Ads.—Abbreviation of word " advertisements," mostly used by news-hands.

Advs.—Another form of abbreviation for the word " advertisements."

Albert envelopes.—Small square envelopes to take Albert notepaper in half, $4\frac{1}{4} \times 3\frac{1}{4}$ inches.

Albert note.—A size of note paper cut $6 \times 3\frac{7}{8}$ inches.

Albertype.—A photographic process of printing.

Albion press.—An improved iron printing hand-press first invented by Mr. Cope.

Aldine.—Printing after the style of Aldus Manutius, the celebrated Venetian printer who invented *italic* types, and flourished in the fifteenth century.

Alexandra press.—An iron printing hand-press after the Albion style.

Algebraical signs.—Marks of expression used in algebra.

All got up.—This term is used when copy is finished, or type is all set up.

All in.—When type is limited and all distributed, it is said to be " all in."

All in hand.—Copy when all given out is said to be " all in hand."

All out.—This term is used when copy or type is exhausted.

All up.—When type is all used, or copy all in type, it is said to be " all up."

Alloy.—The metal of which type is made is an alloy principally of lead, antimony, and tin.

Alterations.—A general term for heavy corrections or the changing of margins.

Altering margin.—Adapting the furniture from one size to another, *i.e.* from small paper to large paper, or *vice versâ*.

*Alum.—A piece of ordinary alum used by compositors for hardening the fingers in distributing.

American hard packing.—This refers to the system of making ready in vogue in America, in contradistinction to the usual style adopted in England.

Ampersand.—The abbreviation or sign for the word " and " thus—& (roman), *&* (italic), ₵ (black letter).

*Ancient customs.—Those customs recognized by long usage.

Anglo-French machine.—A cylindrical printing machine. It is the result of various English and French ideas.

Antiqua.—A German expression for Roman types.

Antiquarian.—A size of drawing paper, 53 × 31 inches.

Antique type.—Founts of old or mediæval character, such as Caslon's.

A. p.—These initials stand for " author's proof."

Apostrophe.—A mark of punctuation used to denote the possessive or to indicate a contraction.

Appearing.—A term used to express (say) the length of a page exclusive of white line—just that part of a page which " appears " in printing.

Applegath machine.—A cylindrical machine first invented by Mr. Applegath in the early part of the present century.

Arab machine.—A small platen machine for jobbing purposes originally made in America.

Arabic figures.—Ordinary figures, roman or italic, thus— 1 2 3 etc., as distinct from roman numerals.

Arbor.—An iron pillar which was used in the Stanhope press to attach the bar-handle to.

Arm.—Any connecting rod between two distinct working parts of a machine.

Artotype.—A photographic process of printing from glass plates.

*Ascending letters.—These are all letters with up-strokes, such as b d h k l.

Asses.—Compositors were thus termed by pressmen by way of retaliation for being called " pigs."

Asterisk.—A mark thus * technically called a star, generally used as a reference mark.

*Astronomical signs.—Marks used in connection with astronomy.

Atlas.—A size of writing or drawing paper, 33 × 26 inches.

Author's proof.—A proof bearing corrections made by the author or editor.

Autography.—This process is the act of transferring writings or drawings from paper to stone.

Axle.—That part of a machine on which a wheel or shaft revolves.

B

Is the first signature of the printer's alphabet (A being used for the preliminary matter, usually done last).

**ACK boxes.**—Is a term applied to the unoccupied boxes of an upper case where there are no small caps or accents.

Back mark.—The back mark of a laying-on board of a printing machine.

Back of a type.—The reverse side to the nick or belly of a type.

Back pages.—The even or "verso" pages of a printed sheet.

Back stay.—Used for checking the running-out of the press from underneath the platen.

Back-up.—Is to reverse the motion of a machine, mostly performed by hand.

Backing metal.—A metal used for the backs of electrotype plates to bring the thickness up to the standard pica, or type-high if required—the electro itself being a mere "shell."

Backs.—Referring to the "back" margin of pages (see "Gutters")—that part of a book which is sewn when bound; sometimes the crosses are thus termed.

*Backside of the forme.—That part of the forme which touches the imposing surface or bed of press.

Bad colour.—Too much or too little ink used—also uneven distribution and rolling.

*Bad copy.—Applied to badly written MSS. and " lean " copy.

Bad lay.—A sheet badly laid or placed in printing—out of the square or centre.

Bad matter.—Term used to indicate type for distribution.

*Bad register.—In printing the second forme if pages do not back correctly.

Bag cap.—A size of brown paper, 24 × 19½ inches.

*Baked.—Applied to type when sticking or caked together, and hard to separate in distributing.

Balaam.—A slang term for standing matter kept for filling up newspapers.

Balaam box.—A slang term for the receptacle containing rejected MSS.

*Ball knife.—A blunt knife which was used for scraping up the old ink-balls.

*Ball leathers.—The outer coverings of the ink-balls were thus described, though not necessarily leather.

Ball linings.—An inner covering used for the old ink-balls.

*Ball nails.—Tacks or clouts used for fastening on the coverings of the old ink-balls.

Ball necks.—That part of the stock of the ink-ball between the handle and the pelt.

Ball racks.—A receptacle for ink-balls out of use.

*Ball stocks.—The handle and body combined used for the old ink-balls.

*Balls.—The old custom of distributing ink was by " balls," rollers being a modern institution.

Band.—A belt or strap for imparting motion from the shaft to a machine.

Bank.—A wooden table or bench for placing the sheets on as printed.

Bank paper.—A thin paper mostly used for foreign letter or note paper to save cost of postage.

Bar.—A cylindrical printing machine with "drop-bar" action for laying on.

Barge.—A small wooden box with six or eight divisions used for holding spaces to alter justification in making corrections. See "Space paper."

Barged case.—When a case is uneven with the various sorts —some full, others empty—it is thus described.

Bastard founts.—A fount of type cast on a larger body than originally intended for. This obviates trouble and the expense of leading a smaller body.

Bastard title.—A fly or half-title before the full title of a work. ·

Batter.—Broken or damaged letter or letters through accident, wear and tear, or carelessness.

Beam engine.—A vertical or perpendicular engine.

Beano.—A slang abbreviation for "beanfeast," which is, however, usually termed "goose" or wayzgoose by compositors.

*Beard of a letter.—The blank sloping part, foot or head, of the shoulder of a type not occupied by the face of the letter.

*Bearer.—A clump or anything type-high to bear off the impression from the light parts of a broken forme.

*Beat.—In order to impart good colour to a particularly solid part of a forme—a woodcut, for instance—a pressman beats that portion with his roller to give it additional ink.

*Beat fat.—To give ample ink in rolling or beating a cut.

*Beat lean.—To insufficiently ink a forme in rolling or inking a cut.

Beater.—A wooden implement used in the warehouse in packing, to make the ends and corners of a parcel lie flat and square.

*Bed.—The table or "coffin" of a machine or press upon which the forme lies.

Bed of the frame.—The lower part of the frame, which forms a shelf that can be used for placing surplus sorts, etc. on.

Begin a fresh par.—To commence a fresh paragraph by means of indentation.

Begin even.—To expedite composition where the copy is in long paragraphs, the compositor starts at random, that is, in the middle of a sentence, and the preceding compositor " makes even " to his " take " of copy.

Bellows.—The ordinary domestic article used for blowing the dust out of cases which have been lying by out of use.

Belly of a type.—The front or nick side of a type.

Belts.—The straps or bands used for driving machinery.

*Benvenue.—A kind of entrance fee paid to the chapel by a workman on entering a fresh office—an old custom. Derived from the French *bienvenue*, welcome.

Bevel wheel.—A cog wheel bevelled to fit into a similar one in driving machinery at right angles.

Bevelled edges.—Book covers and cards are thus termed when the edges are sloped or chamfered.

Bevelled rules.—Rules to properly form a square frame or border must be bevelled at an angle of forty-five degrees.

Bill.—A term for a broadside or poster.

Bill.—Record of work done. Also used to indicate a complete fount of letter cast to a particular scale which type-founders have.

Bills in parliament.—A class of work which has a particular scale of prices in composition.

Bind.—To do up in cloth or otherwise a book or pamphlet.

*Binder.—A short term for a bookbinder.

Bindery.—An Americanism for a bookbinding establishment.

Binding.—In locking-up a forme if the furniture is longer or wider than the type and doubles, it is said to bind, and the pages cannot be tightened up properly.

*****Bite.**—When a page or portion thereof is not printed by reason of the frisket being badly cut out and the impression only shows.

Black and white.—A euphemism for paper and print.

Black letter.—A general expression used to indicate old English, text, or church type.

Bklr.—An abbreviation for "black letter" used by booksellers in cataloguing.

Blacks.—When a space, quadrat, or furniture rises and is imprinted on the sheet. Also used when woodcuts and electros are not sufficiently cleared out, and print the low parts.

Blank page.—Any page of a forme that has no print on.

Blanks.—Blank pages or spaces are sometimes expressed thus.

*****Blankets.**—Flannel or woollen cloth used in the tympans of a press or on the cylinder of a machine. Not used very much now except for old and uneven type—the new system of hard packing being preferred.

Bleed.—When a book or pamphlet has been cut down too much, so as to touch the printed matter.

Blind blocked.—Lettering on book covers not inked or gilt —simply impressed.

Blind P.—A paragraph mark ¶ so called from the loop of the p being closed.

*****Block.**—A general term used—embracing woodcuts, electros, or zincos.

Block books.—The early books of the Chinese were thus called; they were printed entirely from engraved blocks.

Blocked.—This applies to the lettering on cloth book-covers, which is blocked at one operation, not hand-stamped.

Blocked-up.—Type is said to be blocked-up, when owing to author, or over-pressure in press or machine-room, the formes cannot be printed off.

Blotting paper.—Paper of a very soft and absorbent nature —use obvious.

Blow-off pipe.—An outlet pipe at the bottom of a boiler.

Board racks.—Racks, made in "bulks" usually, to hold laying-up boards.

Boards.—A general term for paste and cardboards. A short term for the laying-up boards used by compositors for distribution. Also applied to wetting and glazed boards.

*Bodkin.—A pointed steel instrument fixed in a round handle, mostly used to correct with in the metal.

*Body.—This is the shank of a letter. Also applied to the text or general type of a volume, "body of the work."

Body of the work.—The text or subject-matter of a volume is thus described to distinguish it from the preliminary, appendix, or notes.

Boiler gauge.—A tube to show depth of water in boiler.

Boiler tubes.—The tubes which run at the back of the furnace to carry off the smoke to the shaft.

Bold.—This expression applies to fat-faced type, such as is used in catalogues, etc. See "Clarendon."

Bolster.—A stop at the end of the ribs of the press to prevent the carriage running out too far.

Bolts.—Heads and fore-edge are thus described by the binder in receiving instructions for opening or not opening edges of a book.

Book founts.—Founts of type distinct from fancy or jobbing types.

Book-house.—A printing office where book-work more especially is executed, in contradistinction to a jobbing or news-office.

Booking.—When a book is gathered in sections, on account of the great number of sheets in the volume, and the different sections are afterwards gathered together to form the book, this term is applied.

Booklets.—An affected term for short or small books or pamphlets.

Book press.—The warehouse screw-press which was used, previously to hydraulic presses, for pressing books.

Book quoins.—A medium size of wooden quoin—the larger kind being called "news quoins."

Books (Sizes of).—Various kinds, such as folio, quarto, octavo, sixteenmo, thirty-twomo, etc., which see respectively.

Book-work.—That class of work which is distinct from jobbing or newspaper.

Botanical signs.—Marks of expression used in botany.

*****Botch.**—Bad or careless workmanship. See "Fudge."

Botcher.—A bad or careless workman.

Bottle-arsed.—Type thickened at the feet through wear and tear in continual impression and improper planing down.

Bottle-necked.—Type thicker at the top than the bottom—the reverse of "bottle-arsed."

Bottom boards.—The lower or taking-off boards of a printing machine.

*****Bottom line.**—The last line in a page.

Bottom notes.—Foot-notes are sometimes thus called, to distinguish them from side-notes.

Bound.—The term for books when in covers—cloth or otherwise, as distinct from books in quires.

Bourgeois.—The name of a type one size larger than Brevier and one size smaller than Long Primer—equal to half a Great Primer in body.

*Bowing a letter.—An old expression for breaking and dis-
carding a battered letter.

Bowra rule cutter.—A small rule or lead cutter invented
by Mr. Bowra, and made by Messrs. Harrild and Sons.

Box in.—A term used to indicate that rules should be placed
round as a border.

*Boxes.—The divisions of a type case.

Boxwood shooting stick.—A locking-up stick made of
that particular kind of wood.

Brace pliers.—An implement used for curving brass rule in
making braces.

*Braces. ‿‿ These are cast on their own bodies and by
degrees of ems, and used to connect lines.   Longer ones are
usually made of brass rule by special pliers.

Bracket.—A holder or hanger from the roof to support
shafting.

Bracket.—A sign of punctuation, thus [or]

Brake.—Apparatus for facilitating the stopping of machinery.

Branch out.—To lead or " white " out a title or display lines
of any kind.

Brass circles.—These are used for jobbing purposes, such
as seals, trade marks, etc., and made oval or round, but generally called circles.

Brass composing rules.—In order to expedite the setting
of type compositors use a rule which is shifted line by line.
They are sometimes made of steel.

Brass curves.—Curves used for shaping the lines of type in
display work—either circular or semicircular.

Brass face.—Electrotypes are brass faced to prevent red ink
turning dirty, when it is requisite to print in that colour.

*Brass rules.—Used for borders and lines in columns, etc.,
and cast to different thicknesses.

Brass rules (Varieties of).—There are several kinds, such as dotted, wavy, plain, double, thick, thin, etc.

***Bray.**—This is to distribute ink on the table by means of the brayer, preparatory to taking it on the roller.

***Brayer.**—A wooden implement for rubbing out ink on the table for fresh distribution.

Brayer ink table.—A table used by pressmen on which to bray ink out, distinct from cylindrical ink tables.

***Break.**—An expression used to indicate the end or commencement of a paragraph. It is also indicated in copy by a bracket mark, thus [or]

***Break.**—To pie or "squash" type.

***Break of a letter.**—The surplus metal on the foot of a letter as cast from the mould.

Break up.—An amateurish expression for distribute or clear away.

Break up into pars.—To break up solid copy into short paragraphs.

Bremner machines.—Various platen and cylindrical machines invented by Mr. Samuel Bremner.

***Brevier.**—A size of type one size larger than Minion and one size smaller than Bourgeois.

Brevier brass rule.—Brass rules cast on a Brevier body.

Brilliant.—A size of type one size larger than Minnikin and one size smaller than Gem.

Bring up.—To make ready or level the type by overlaying or patching up.

Bristol boards.—A class of very fine pasteboards chiefly used for drawing purposes.

Broad.—A piece of furniture, wood or metal, four picas in width.

Broad and narrow.—Furniture seven picas in width—a broad and narrow combined.

Broad quotations.—Metal quotations four ems pica square.

Broad thirds card.—A "large" card cut into three the long way.

*Broadside.—A sheet printed one side only, such as a poster or bill.

Broadside composing stick.—A long implement specially made of wood for lightness.

Broadside chases.—Large chases without cross-bars used for this class of work.

*Broken letter.—Is said of type pied or squabbled.

Broken matter.—See " Broken letter."

Broken neck.—When the handle of the old ink-ball stock was broken, it was thus described.

Bronze ink.—Various inks made with an addition of bronze. When dry, they give a decided metallic appearance to the surface.

Bronze preparation.—A varnish used for printing, preparatory to dusting the bronze on the impressed letters.

Bronze printing.—The art of printing in bronze.

Bronzing machine.—A mechanical contrivance to economize time and obviate waste of material.

Brooks' press.—An improved Stanhope press invented by Mr. Brooks in the early part of this century.

Browns.—A technical term used to describe the make of paper known as " brown paper."

Brush out.—To clean out a forme by means of lye or turpentine.

Bulk.—Usually the bench situated at the end of a composing frame.

Bullet.—When a workman is discharged without notice he is said to have "got the bullet." Sometimes it is used when he receives notice to leave in the usual manner.

Bullock press.—One of the original Web printing machines of American make, called after a person of that name.

Bullock's heart.—Pressmen's expression for 250 copies working—a " lean " number.

Bundle.—Usually means two reams of paper in a parcel.

***Bur.**—The roughness left on a letter through insufficient dressing by the type-founder.

Burnished edges.—When edges are coloured and polished with a burnisher.

Business cards.—The class of cards used in commercial circles denoting one's business, name, and address.

Button of tympan.—The stud on the frame which the hook catches in order to hold the inner and outer tympans secure.

Button on.—A slang term sometimes used by printers for a workman with " a fit of the blues."

C

Is the second signature of the printer's alphabet.

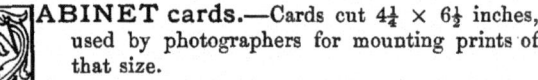

ABINET cards.—Cards cut $4\frac{1}{4}$ × $6\frac{1}{2}$ inches, used by photographers for mounting prints of that size.

Calendered paper. — Paper very highly rolled or glazed, much used for the printing of illustrated books or magazines.

Calendering.—Rolling or glazing of paper is thus described.

Cam.—A wheel of irregular shape (not round) to impart eccentric motion to any particular part of a machine.

Cambric.—This material was formerly used instead of parchment for covering tympans in fine presswork.

Campbell machine.—A single cylinder machine of American make.

Cancel.—A reprint of a leaf or leaves owing to a mistake—literary or technical—and usually indicated by an asterisk in the white line.

*Canon.—A type four picas deep in body, but somewhat small in face.

*Capitals.—Letters other than lower case or small capitals.

Caps.—Abbreviation of word " capitals," and usually indicated by three lines ≣ in MS.

Caps and smalls.—A word or words set in small capitals with the initial letter a full capital—thus, Printer—indicated by three and two underlinings respectively, thus ≣ and ≇ in copy.

Carbon paper.—Black manifold paper used by drapers and others for duplicating invoices, etc.

Cardboard.—Boards made, sometimes of pulp, and sometimes of sheets pasted together, and afterwards rolled.

Card chases.—Small chases used for cards or similar small jobs.

Card-cutting machine.—A small machine specially made for the cutting of cards.

Card machine.—A small treadle—sometimes worked by steam-power—for the printing of cards or other small jobs.

Card press.—A small jobbing hand-press—treadle machines are sometimes so called—used for printing cards or other small work.

Cards.—General term for paste or pulp boards. This term is often applied to the various sizes cut from the boards.

Cards (Sizes of).—There are several regular sizes, such as large, small, thirds, town, cabinet, carte de visite, etc., which see respectively.

Caret.—Marked thus ∧ to indicate an insertion in copy.

*Carriage.—The bed or coffin on which the forme is laid and which runs under the platen or cylinder in a printing press or machine.

Carte de visite cards.—Cards cut 4½ × 2½ inches, used by photographers for mounting prints of that size.

Cartridge paper.—A machine-made paper exceptionally hard-sized.

*Case.—The receptacle in which type is laid to compose from. When in pairs, defined as upper and lower respectively.

Case barged.—An uneven case of type—some boxes empty, others full or nearly so.

Case department.—That portion of a printing office occupied by the compositors.

c

*Case is full.—When the case has been filled by distribution or laying of new type.

*Case is low.—When the type has been nearly all set out.

Case overseer.—The foreman of the composing department.

Case racks.—Receptacles for holding cases when out of use —distinct from frame racks, which are used for cases in use.

Case runs over.—When the case has been over-filled.

Case work.—A term for publishers' or cloth binding.

Case work.—The general expression for defining the compositors' work in printing a book.

Cases.—An expression generally applied to cloth book-covers.

Cases down.—When cases are out of use and taken down from the frame, the fact is thus expressed.

Cases up.—When cases are in use and up on the frame, the fact is thus expressed, in contradistinction to " cases down."

Casing.—A size of brown paper, 46 × 36 inches.

Casing paper.—A machine-made paper which comes under the head of " browns "—used for wrapping purposes.

Caslon type.—A term sometimes applied to the old-faced types cut by William Caslon.

*Cassie paper.—Outside or broken paper was formerly thus spoken of.

*Cast.—Generally applied to a stereotype cast.

Cast-iron chases.—Chases made by casting in an iron foundry. These, though cheaper than wrought iron, are rougher and more likely to be fractured if not carefully handled.

*Cast-off.—To calculate or estimate length of copy to be printed—a troublesome task in uneven and badly-written MS.

Casting-up.—To measure the pages by means of ems and ens of its own body according to the existing scale of prices.

Catches.—Made generally of brass, to hold stereo or electrotype plates on blocks.

Catchline.—The line which contains the "catchword" at the bottom of a page.

Catchword.—A word placed at the bottom right-hand corner of pages in old books, indicating the first word on the following page.

Cater-cornered.—Sheets of paper when not cut square.

Caxton.—The particular kind of Old English type used for composing books in that character.

Caxton cases.—Cases of special lay for composing works in that character, by reason of the many ligatures.

Caxton machine.—A small platen jobbing machine worked by foot or by steam-power, made by Messrs. Furnival and Co., Stockport.

Cedilla c.—A French accent—thus, ç

Celluloid.—A composition made principally, it is said, of refuse from gun-cotton. Plates have been cast from type in this material, and as it is very hard it is admirably adapted for tint blocks.

Centred figures.—Small-faced figures cast centrally on a larger body, generally used in numbering lines for reference purposes in poetical works.

Ceriphs.—The fine strokes at the ends of letters—thus, H which do not appear in *sans* ceriphs—H

Certificate.—A guarantee of a limited number of copies only having been printed of any work, usually placed near the title-page.

Chaostype.—A particular kind of type of a fantastic character.

*Chapels.—The meetings held by the workmen to consider trade affairs, appeals, and other matters are thus termed. Derived, it is said, from Caxton's connection with Westminster Abbey.

Chapelonians.—Members of any chapel in a printing office.

Chapel money.—An ancient custom of allowing pecuniary commission by the tradesmen to members of a chapel. A reprehensible practice nowadays, however.

Chapel rules.—Most chapels, press or compositors', have a set of rules for the guidance of their members.

Chapter heads.—The headings at the top of a chapter.

Chart paper.—A machine-made paper manufactured of best rags, specially adapted for charts and maps, being strong in texture and thin for folding purposes.

*Chase.—An iron frame, cast or wrought, to hold the type for printing.

Chases (Varieties of).—Several kinds, such as cast- or wrought-iron, folding, folio, quarto, jobbing, etc.

Check book.—A tabulated book used by compositors to show at a glance the progress of a work, and also by which to check the composition and charges thereon.

Check screw.—A screw in the hand-press to regulate the length of pull.

*Cheeks.—The upright sides of a printing press, between which the carriage or bed is run before pulling the bar over.

Chemical signs.—Marks of expression used in chemistry.

Cheque papers.—Generally hand-made from best rags, and as a rule specially water-marked.

Chill.—An elbow of steel immediately at the end of the press bar, which gives the impression by its being moved into a vertical position on the bar being pulled over.

Chinese paper.—A thin paper of very soft texture used by engravers to pull proofs on. Erroneously called " India " paper.

Chinese white.—A colourless pigment used for thinning or blending coloured inks.

*Choked.—An expression used when the face of type gets filled up with ink and dirt, owing to bad washing and rinsing of formes.

Chopper on.—A person with a fit of " the blues " and intensely miserable is thus described. It is a slang expression sometimes used by printers.

Chromograph.—A copying process by means of writing on a preparation of gelatine, etc., whereby a large number of copies may be printed.

Chromo-lithography.—The art of printing in colours by lithography.

Circled corrections.—Special alterations made after the type has been corrected are generally encircled on the proof in order to call particular attention to them.

Circles.—Brass rings cast hollow to allow of type being placed inside.

Circuit edges.—Books, generally bibles or prayer-books, are sometimes bound with the covers projecting and turned over to protect the edges.

Circular saw.—A revolving saw used for cutting up plates, furniture, etc.

Circulars.—The class of small job work which includes letters, circulars, etc.

*Circumflex.—Accented letters marked thus, â ê î ô û

City printing machine.—A single-cylinder machine made by Mr. Ingle.

Clarendon.—A bold or fat-faced type is generally thus described ; the older founts were called " Egyptian."

*Claw.—The tail of a sheepsfoot.

Claws.—Another name for the catches of stereotype blocks ; usually made of brass, but sometimes of steel.

*Clean proof.—A term used to discriminate between a foul or first proof and a proof ready to be sent out to a customer.

Clean sheets.—Sheets put aside as printed off to show progress of work and for editorial purposes.

Clean up.—To clean or wipe up machinery when idle.

Clearing away.—A term applied to express literally clearing away the type of a job or work after printing, *i.e.* to unlead, take headlines, etc., away, and tie up in pieces, preparatory to papering-up and storing.

Clearing pie.—To separate and distribute broken or mixed type into their proper cases.

Clearing stone.—After correcting a forme it is a rule in all well-ordered offices for the compositor to put away all stray letters and tools into their proper places. A fine is customary in some offices for breaking this rule.

Clerical errors.—Mistakes in copying MS.

Clerk of the chapel.—Practically the secretary of a chapel, who collects the subscriptions, etc.

Cliché.—French term for a cast, usually applied to stereo or electro duplicates.

Clicker.—The compositor in charge of a companionship, who receives copy and instructions direct from the overseer or principal, and is responsible to his companions for the charging of the work done.

Clicking.—The system of working in companionships under a clicker.

*Close matter.—Matter with few breaks, and set solid, *i.e.* without leads. See "Lean" and "Solid dig."

Close spacing.—By this is meant spacing less than a thick space. Works not leaded should be rather more closely spaced than leaded ones.

*Close work.—See "Close matter."

Closed apostrophes.—Double apostrophes (") used to indicate the end of any quoted passage.

Closed office.—A printing office closed to " society " hands.

Closed up.—When a compositor has been behindhand with his share of copy and his companions awaiting the completion, he is said to have " closed up " when finished.

Closet.—The counting-house is sometimes thus described, as is also the reading-room. See " The closet."

Cloth boards.—Books when bound in cloth cases are described as being in " cloth boards."

Cloth-faced paper.—Paper and cloth or linen pasted together, used especially for folding cards to prevent the score breaking.

Clothing rollers.—Changing the composition on worn-out rollers.

Clumps.—Metal furniture, or pieces of metal used by stereo-typers, etc., chiefly to form the bevel of a plate.

Clymer press.—An iron hand-press called the Columbian made by Mr. Clymer of Philadelphia, who came to England in the early part of this century.

Cobb paper.—A paper largely used by bookbinders for the sides of half-bound books. It is made in various shades of colour.

Cock.—In throwing or "jeffing" with quadrats as dice, when one lodges on top of another—thus lifting it partly off the surface thrown on—it is thus termed. Another throw is then allowed.

Cock-robin shop.—A small printing office where common work is done, and labour is badly paid for, is generally thus described.

Cock-up.—A superior figure or letter that does not range at bottom, and is used for contractions, thus " M^r. " or " A^1."

*Coffin.—The carriage or bed of a cylindrical machine or platen press.

Coffin.—A little conical bag, made of paper, to put sorts in—similar to those made by grocers for sugar, etc.

Cogger's press.—An old iron hand-press invented by Mr. T. Cogger in the early part of this century.

Cog-wheels.—Wheels with teeth for transmitting motion from one part of a machine to another.

Cold pressing.—Sheets pressed between glazed boards, usually, and more effectually, in a hydraulic press.

Cold rolling.—In contradistinction to hot rolling—the rollers being made hot in the one instance, and in the other the rollers being in the natural state.

Collar.—A circular band fastened with nuts and screws to hold two lengths of shafting together.

*Collate.—To run through the sheets of a book to see if the signatures are in sequence.

Colombier.—A drawing paper, size 34½ × 23½ inches.

Colon.—A mark of punctuation :

Co.—Abbreviation of the word "colon," used in the reading department.

Colophon.—An inscription or tailpiece—usually a printer's imprint—at the end of a book.

Colour printing.—Printing in one or more colours than black is thus termed.

Coloured edges.—The edges of books when other than simply cut or gilt.

Columbian press.—An iron hand-press invented by Mr. Clymer of Philadelphia in the early part of this century.

Column galley.—A metal galley used in newspaper work.

Column matter.—Type set in two or more columns is thus described.

Column rules.—Rules used for dividing columns in double-columned work or newspapers.

Come in.—When copy is got into a given space it is said to "come in."

*Come off.—A sheet as printed is said to "come off" easily, or the reverse, if difficult to leave the forme by reason of heavy cuts.

Comma.—A mark of punctuation ,

Com.—Abbreviation of the word "comma," used in the reading department.

Commence turns.—Reversed double commas (") used to indicate the commencement of any quoted passage.

Commercial envelopes.—Envelopes to take large post 8vo in three, $5\frac{1}{2} \times 3\frac{1}{4}$ inches.

Commercial signs.—Marks of expression used by commercial persons, such as £ @ ℔ $

Common points.—Ordinary points with a pin or spur attached, in contradistinction to "spring points," etc.

*Companions.—Two men who work at a press are thus styled, as also the members of a companionship, or body of compositors working together under a clicker.

Comp.—Abbreviation for companion or compositor, much used by compositors.

Companionship.—A number of compositors who work together under a clicker.

Comping.—A slang term for composing or setting type.

Complete fount.—A fount of type including capitals, small capitals, lower-case, figures, accents, spaces, etc., as distinct from "sorts."

*Compose.—To set up type.

Composing machines.—Mechanical appliances for setting type. Various kinds have been invented from time to time with more or less success.

Composing room (or department).—The portion of a printing office occupied by the compositors.

*Composing rule.—A brass rule, with a nose-piece, the length of the measure or width of the type being set up; it facilitates the composition in being shifted line by line.

*Composing stick.—A tool or implement for setting type in, usually made of iron or gun-metal. Long sticks, such as are used for broadsides, are made of wood for lightness.

Composition.—Rollers made principally of glue and treacle.

Compo.—Abbreviation for the roller composition.

Composition.—The art of composing or setting type.

*Compositor.—A type-setter or composer of type.

Compositors' rules.—Type measures or scales made of boxwood or ivory.

Compound words.—Two words of equal grammatical value joined by a hyphen.

Condensed letter.—Thin and elongated founts of type are thus described.

Condition.—Rollers are said to be in or out of condition according to their merits.

Conditions of sale.—The class of legal work embracing conditions and particulars of sale.

Connection.—In passing sheets of a work finally for press the reader sees that the sequence from sheet to sheet is preserved, and not disturbed by any overrunning.

Con.—Abbreviation of the word " connection," used in the reading department.

Contents.—That part of the preliminary matter which gives the " contents " and pagination of the various sections of a work.

Contractions.—Abbreviations, or record sorts, indicated by accents over or through the letters.

Cope's press.—This is the Albion iron hand-press invented by Mr. Cope.

*Copy.—The manuscript or reprint copy from which the compositor composes.

Copyholder.—The reading " boy " in a newspaper office.

*Copy money.—In olden times each compositor received a copy of the work he had been employed on, or a pecuniary reward. The custom is now obsolete.

Copy paper.—A writing paper, size 20 × 16 inches.

Copyright.—The rights held by publisher or author for a certain term of years in any original work.

Copy's out.—When the copy is all in hand, but not necessarily all composed, it is said to be "out."

Copying paper.—A thin paper used for copying letters and accounts in commercial circles.

Copper bronze.—Bronze powder made of copper used for printing purposes.

Copper-faced.—Casts—really electrotypes—are thus described, to distinguish them from stereotypes.

Copperplate printing.—The art of intaglio printing from engraved copper-plates.

*Cording quires.—The outside quires of a ream, generally called " outsides."

Cores.—Metal stereo blocks cast on girder-like sections to reduce weight of forme and economize metal.

Corks.—A slang expression sometimes used by printers to express money.

Corner irons.—The corner pieces of iron screwed on the corners of the bed or coffin of a press.

Corner-up.—A sheet or sheets when doubled up at the corners is said to be cornered up.

Corners.—An ornament used for decorating the corner of a border in brass rule or otherwise.

Corners rounded.—Cards are supplied with the corners rounded.

*Correct.—To amend errors or make alterations in a proof.

Correcting nippers.—A pair of tweezers used for correcting type—especially handy for tabular work.

*Correcting stone.—The surface on which a forme is laid to be corrected. See "Imposing stone."

*Corrections.—The emendations or alterations made on a proof.

*Corrector.—An ancient term for a reader, now called " corrector of the press," the term used by the Readers' Association.

Corrigenda.—Plural of " corrigendum " (Latin), corrections of errors, etc.

Corrigendum.—Singular of " corrigenda."

Cotton waste.—Refuse cotton used as " wipings " to clean machinery, etc.

Counter.—The person responsible for the proper counting of all work as it is printed off.

Counter shafting.—A smaller shaft connected with the main shaft in driving machinery.

*Counting off copy.—See " Casting off."

Court envelopes.—Square envelopes to take large or small post 8vo in half, and termed respectively " large" or " small " court.

*Cramped.—When matter is set close and insufficiently " whited out."

Crank.—A long arm connected with a wheel or cam, with a backward or forward motion.

Cream-laid.—A writing paper showing the wire marks when held up.

Cream-wove.—A writing paper without wire marks—the reverse of " cream-laid."

Creamy paper.—Paper with a slight tone is thus described.

Creswick.—A handmade drawing paper so called after the person of that name.

Cropped.—A book is said to be " cropped " when cut down too much.

Cropper machine.—An American small treadle platen machine made by Mr. Cropper. The original one was the " Minerva."

Cropper.—A short term for the " cropper " small printing platen machine.

*Cross-bars.—The bars which divide chases into sections—fixed in cast chases, but generally movable in wrought ones.

*Crosses.—The cross-bars of chases are familiarly thus called.

*Crotchets.—Another expression for brackets [or] somewhat out of date.

Crowded.—When type is composed somewhat close or cramped it is said to be " crowded."

Crown.—A size of printing paper, 20 × 15 inches.

Crystallotypy.—A process of producing artificial crystallized tint plates.

*Cull paper.—To examine and select the best of damaged paper.

Curly ñ.—A term for the accented letter used in record work or in Spanish.

Currying irons.—These were used for currying the old ink balls, *i.e.* taking the moisture out of the ball.

Curvilinear plates.—Special stereo plates curved, cast, and bent for cylinder machines, as used for newspapers.

Custom of the house.—Certain rules and regulations in vogue in any particular printing office.

Cut away.—To lower or cut away any particular part in a making-ready sheet.

Cut down.—An expression used when paper is cut from one size to another.

Cut edges.—A book which has been cut all round is said to have cut edges.

Cut formes.—Formes of illustrations, in contradistinction to ordinary formes of type or bookwork.

Cut-in letter.—A two-line or larger letter inserted at the commencement of a chapter.

Cut-in notes.—Side-notes which are inserted within the text at the side, instead of in the margin.

Cut out.—To cut out an overlay, or cut away in a making-ready sheet.

Cut size.—An indefinite or irregular size, not a recognized size of paper.

Cut the line.—Companionships "cut the line," *i.e.* cease work, when there is insufficient to keep the whole "ship" going.

Cut up.—A warehouse expression for cutting up paper to certain sizes, such as used for jobs, *i.e.* 8vo, 4to, etc.

Cuts.—This is a colloquial expression for an illustration of any kind—electrotype, woodcut, or zincograph.

Cutter.—The person in the warehouse who does the cutting.

Cutting-out knife.—A sharp-pointed knife used in making ready.

*Cutting the frisket.—To cut the printing portions of a forme out of the frisket.

Cylinder bearers.—The sides of the coffin or bed of the machine, made of hard wood, type-high.

Cylinder galley press.—A small press for pulling galley proofs by means of a heavy roller or cylinder pushed along by hand.

Cylinder machine.—A printing machine giving the impression by a cylinder instead of a platen.

Cylinder sheets.—The sheets pasted upon the cylinder which form the foundation of the making-ready.

Cylindrical ink table.—An ink table which revolves by a handle, and thus gives the ink to the roller, instead of braying out by the tool for the purpose.

D

Is the third signature of the printer's alphabet.

AGGER.—A mark of reference used for foot-notes, thus †

Damper.—A door placed in the flue from the furnace to the upright shaft to regulate the draught.

*Dances.—An old expression applied when the spaces or quadrats rise in printing.

Dandy.—The wire frame or mould on which paper is made.

Dash.—A mark used in punctuation, thus — technically called metal rule.

Dead languages.—The classical languages, which are not now generally spoken.

Decimo-sexto.—The bibliographical term for sixteenmo—written shortly, 16mo.

Deckle.—The raw, rough edge of paper in hand-mades is thus termed.

*Dele.—To omit or expunge, indicated thus δ It is derived from the Latin.

Demy.—A size of printing paper, $22\frac{1}{2} \times 17\frac{1}{2}$ inches; writing paper, $20 \times 15\frac{1}{2}$ inches.

*Descending letters.—These are all those letters with down strokes, thus—p q y, etc.

*Devil, printer's.—An odd lad for errands and other jobs—sometimes the junior apprentice is thus called.

Dextrine.—A cheap substitute for gum.

*Diæresis.—An accent mark over letters, thus—ä ë ï ö ü

Diamond.—The type one size larger than Gem, and one size smaller than Pearl—equal to half a Bourgeois in body.

Dictionary matter.—A class of composition which has a special price.

Die stamping.—The art of stamping in relief, as used for note paper or envelopes.

*Direction.—The corner word in the white line to indicate the first word on next page. See " Catchword."

*Direction line.—The bottom line in a page containing the catchword.

Dirty proof.—A proof-sheet with many corrections due to careless composition.

Display work.—Type displayed, such as titles, headings, and jobbing work, is thus termed to distinguish it from ordinary solid composition.

*Distribute.—To replace the type in cases after printing. See " Dis."

Dis.—Abbreviation of the word " distribute."

Distributing rollers.—The rollers which take the ink from the vibrator communicating with the ductor. The rollers have a diagonal movement, and distribute the ink on the table. They are sometimes called " wavers."

Divide.—To separate a word at the end of a line with a hyphen.

*Division.—See " Divide."

*Divisorium.—An article used for holding copy on the case, which will allow of the copy being adjusted line by line to avoid " outs" or " doubles." See " Visorum."

Do up.—A general term for folding, stitching, and wrappering, or binding in cloth.

Doc.—A slang term for the weekly bill, evidently a curtailment of " document."

Dog's-eared.—When the corners of a ream of paper are curled or knocked up.

Dollar mark.—A sign used in American currency, thus $

Donkey engine.—A small and subsidiary engine apart from the main one.

Donkeys.—Compositors were at one period thus styled by pressmen in retaliation for being called " pigs " by them.

Doric fount.—A particular kind of sans-serif type used for display work.

Dotted figures.—Special figures cast with a dot above—i̇ 2̇ 3̇ etc.

Dotted letters.—Special letters cast with a dot above, thus— ȧ ė i̇ ȯ u̇ etc.

Dotted quadrats.—Dots or full-points cast on quadrats, generally called " leaders," thus ... ... used for contents or table matter to run out to figures.

Dotted rule.—Brass rule with the face dotted, used for filling up blanks, receipt forms, etc., and to serve as a guide for writing on, thus ·····························

*Double.—Words repeated in composition by error, necessitating overrunning; also used by pressmen when a sheet is pulled twice or mackled.

Double broad.—Furniture eight picas in width—double the width of " broad."

Double cases.—Cases specially made upper and lower case in one, used for small jobbing founts.

Double columns.—Matter set in two columns.

Double crown.—A size of printing paper, 30 × 20 inches.

Double dagger.—A reference mark for foot-notes, thus ‡

Double demy.—A size of printing paper, 35 × 22½ inches.

Double foolscap.—A size of printing paper, 27 × 17 inches; writing paper, 26½ × 16⅝ inches.

Double four pound.—A size of brown paper, 31 × 22 inches.

Double frame.—A frame to hold two pairs of cases up at one time.

Double imperial.—A size of printing paper, 44 × 30 inches.

Double imperial cap.—A size of brown paper, 44 × 29 inches.

Double large cards.—A size of jobbing card, cut 6 × 4½ inches.

Double large post.—A size of writing paper, 33 × 21 inches.

***Double letters.**—Diphthongs and old-face letters, æ, œ, ﬅ, ct, etc., are thus called.

Double medium.—A size of printing paper, 38 × 24 inches.

Double narrow.—Furniture six picas in width—double the width of a narrow.

***Double pica.**—The name of a fount one size larger than Paragon, and one size smaller than Two-line Pica—its body is two Small Picas in depth.

Double pica reglet.—Wooden furniture of that depth in body.

Double post.—A size of printing paper, usually 32 × 20 inches.

Double pott.—A size of printing paper, 25½ × 17 inches.

Double rolling.—The action of twice rolling a forme in printing by means of a throw-off impression in a machine.

Double royal.—A size of printing paper, 40 × 25 inches.

Double rule.—Rules which are cast with two lines on the face—both in brass and in type metal.

Double small cards.—A size of jobbing card, cut 3½ × 5 inches.

Double small post.—A size of writing paper, 30½ × 19 inches.

Double super royal.—A size of printing paper, 41 × 27½ inches.

Drachm mark.—A medical sign, thus ℥

Drag.—When a shake or slur is on a printed sheet it is said to " drag."

Draw.—When through bad justification the letters draw out on the roller in inking the forme.

Drawing.—Lifting lines from a page or forme for a second printing in another colour—the blank space being filled with its equivalent.

Drawing paper.—A paper, generally hand-made, manufactured of the finest material and well sized.

Drawing paper reams.—These papers are usually done up 472 sheets to a mill ream, with outsides—if all good sheets, that is insides, 480.

Drawn sheets.—Used to indicate sheets drawn in collating gathered books, through carelessness in gathering two or three sheets at a time instead of one.

*****Dress a forme.**—To put furniture round and quoin up a forme, preparatory to pulling a proof.

*****Dressing block.**—An obsolete term for the present planer.

*****Driers.**—A preparation used for increasing the drying properties of inks.

Dripping pan.—A tin tray under the ribs of the press to catch the surplus oil.

*****Drive out.**—To widely space matter.   See " Get in."

Driving band.—The strap or band which imparts motion to a machine.

Driving shaft.—The shaft which imparts motion, through the medium of the strap, to a machine.

Dropped head.—Chapter or first pages driven down at the top are thus called.

Dropping out.—When, owing to long standing or the prevalence of hot weather, the quoins of a forme get loose and the pages drop out of the chase.

Drum.—Another term for the "cylinder" of a printing machine.

Dry up.—A slang term for leaving off work or leaving a situation.

Dryden machine.—A perfecting printing machine manufactured by a firm of that name.

Duck's bill.—A substitute for pins in a tympan, made by cutting a tongue in a piece of thick paper or card.

Ductor.—A reservoir which holds the ink in a printing machine, the supply from it being regulated for each impression.

Duct.—Abbreviation of the word "ductor."

Ductor keys.—Screws placed in the ductor to regulate the amount of ink to be given to each impression.

Ductor knife.—The long thin plate which regulates the amount of ink given out for every impression.

Duodecimo.—Commonly called twelvemo, a sheet of paper folded into twelve leaves, written shortly, 12mo.

Duplex cards.—Pasteboards, the two surfaces of different colours.

Duplex paper.—Paper with the two sides of different colours, made by colouring each side separately.

Dutch papers.—Van Gelder's handmade paper of various sizes, made in Holland.

Dwell.—The stationary period while a sheet is being impressed on the type or forme—a long "dwell" is a good point in a machine.

E

Is the fourth signature of the printer's alphabet.

EAR of the frisket.*—The thumb-piece used in turning down the frisket on the tympan.

***Easy pull.**—A soft or easy pull over of the handle of a press.

Eccentric motion.—A movement of irregular action which acts on a certain part of a machine at a particular moment in an evolution.

Ecclesiastic.—A particular fount of type of black letter or church text character.

Edges bevelled.—Cards or book-covers with the edges bevelled to any degree.

Edges cut.—A book or pamphlet cut down sufficiently to make all the edges quite smooth.

Edges gilt.—Book edges cut and gilded.

Edges opened.—A book or pamphlet opened with a paper knife by hand.

Edges red.—Book edges cut and coloured red.

Edges rounded.—Books are sometimes bound with the corners rounded to prevent them becoming " dog's-eared."

Edges trimmed.—A book or pamphlet with the edges just cut to make them tidy, but not sufficiently to open the leaves.

Edges untouched.—A book or pamphlet with edges uncut or unopened.

Edition de luxe.—French colloquialism for the large paper editions issued of first-class books.

Egyptian.—A fat and ugly-faced kind of type. There is nowadays a larger and more graceful selection of these fancy types to be chosen from.

*Eighteenmo.—A sheet folded into eighteen leaves. See "Octodecimo," written shortly, 18mo.

Eighteenmo chases.—Chases with the cross-bars divided into four unequal sections to allow of the off-cut.

*Eights.—A familiar term used by compositors for octavo.

Eight to pica brass.—Brass rule cast eight to a pica in thickness.

Eight to pica leads.—Leads cast eight to a pica; also called "thin" leads.

Elbow point.—Press points made upon an elbow for convenience in pointing twelve or eighteenmo works.

Electrotyping.—The art of duplicating woodcuts, etc., by a thin galvanic deposit of copper, afterwards backed up by ordinary metal similar to that used by type, but not so hard.

Elephant.—A size of printing paper, 30 × 23 inches; writing or drawing paper, 28 × 23 inches; brown paper, 34 × 24 inches.

Elongated.—A thin and condensed form of fancy display type.

Elzevirs.—A class of books named after the eminent Dutch printers of the seventeenth century.

*Em quads.—A quadrat cast one em square to any particular body.

Em rules.—Rules cast on an em of any particular body—a dash, or metal rule.

Embossed printing.—Raised printing instead of the ordinary indented printing—such as die stamping.

Embossing press.—A machine for raised or embossed stamping.

Emerald.—The name of a fount one size larger than Nonpareil and one size smaller than Minion—equal to half an English in body.

Emery cloth.—Used for burnishing the bright parts of machinery.

Emperor.—A size of writing or drawing paper, 72 × 48 inches.

Empire machine.—A small platen machine made by Messrs. Powell and Co.

*Emptied.—When a composing stick or galley is full, and the type is lifted out of the stick or off the galley, it is said to be emptied.

*Empty case.—A case with the type nearly all set out.

*Empty press.—An unemployed press—that is, one standing idle.

*En quads.—Spaces two to an em of any particular body.

En rules.—Rules cast on an en of any particular body.

Enamelled cards.—Cards made with a very high surface by being enamelled on one or both sides.

Enamelled paper.—Paper with a specially prepared surface.

Encircled corrections.—Special or "after" corrections made in a proof, and encircled in order to distinguish them from the corrections first made.

End at a break.—To finish in composing at the end of a paragraph.

End even.—To finish off copy in composing at the end of a line—a plan adopted in order to expedite composition by giving out short "takes."

End leaves.—The blank flyleaves at either end of a book.

End papers.—See "End leaves."

Endless paper.—Paper in reels—not in sheets—used for printing on rotary machines.

Endorse.—The outside endorsement of a prospectus or legal document, when folded.

Engine-sized paper.—Paper sized in process of manufacture, distinct from hand or tub-sized.

*English.—The name of a type one size larger than Pica and one size smaller than Great Primer—equal to two Emeralds in body.

*English face.—An old term for Old English or black letter.

Equal mark.—A sign used in arithmetic, thus =

Equivalent weights of paper.—The difference in weight between two sizes to compensate for a larger or smaller sheet.

Errata.—A number of mistakes usually printed on a small slip and pasted in by the bookbinder. The word is the Latin equivalent for "errors."

Erratum.—The singular of "errata."

Errors.—Blunders in composition, or marks of corrections in proofs.

Establishment.—A workman on weekly wages is said to be on the "establishment." See "'Stab."

Even folios.—The pagination of left-hand pages,—2, 4, 6, 8, 10, etc. are said to be "even folios."

*Even pages.—The even numbers in paging, or left-hand pages of a work. See "Even folios."

Exhaust pipe.—The pipe which conveys away the waste steam.

Exhaust steam.—Waste or spent steam is thus termed.

Expanded.—A fancy type of extended character—the reverse of condensed.

Extended.—Another term for expanded letter.

Extras.—The charges involved on composition over and above the fixed price per sheet of the text type, generally charged at the end of a work.

Eyletting machine.—A machine for punching and inserting the eylets in showcards, etc.

F

Is the fifth signature of the printer's alphabet.

FACE of a letter.*—The surface of a letter—that which is imprinted on the paper.

Faced rule.—Brass rule with the ordinary thin face somewhat thickened.

Facsimile.—To imitate exactly in reprinting—applied generally to reprints of old works.

Facsim.—Abbreviation of the word "facsimile."

Fair offices.—A term applied to those printing offices where the recognized scale of prices is paid.

Falling out.—The quoins of formes which have been long standing in chase are apt to shrink, especially in hot weather, and cause the type to "fall out."

Fancy rules.—Rules other than plain ones of various designs—some short, as used between sections, and border rules.

Fancy types.—Founts of type of various kinds used for jobbing purposes.

Fanning.—In order to count paper it is necessary to open the edges by grasping with the thumb and forefinger two or three quires, and to turn the same over by a sharp turn of the wrist.

*Fat.—Well-leaded, open, or good paying work for piece hands. Sometimes vulgarly called "grease."

*Fat face.—A broad or fat-faced character of type.

*Father of the chapel.—The person who presides at the printers' chapel.

Father.—Short term for " father of the chapel."

Feed pipe.—The pipe which feeds the boiler with water direct from the cistern.

Feeder.—The lad who lays on the sheets in a printing machine.

*Feet of a press.—The bottom of the legs of a press resting on the ground. .

Feint ruling.—Very light and thin lines used in account ruling.

Fellow-comp.—A term of fellowship applied by one compositor to another.

Fellow-P.—Apprentices to the same firm or master.

Fence.—A guard or railing round dangerous machinery or bands.

Filigree letter.—An initial letter with a filigree background.

Filling in.—Putting the sheets, after printing and drying, between glazed boards previous to pressing.

Fine presswork.—A term applied to the better class of handwork in printing.

Fingers.—The grippers which hold the paper in printing on a machine.

Fire bars.—The bars which form the bottom of a furnace. They are renewable when worn out by the heat.

Fire door.—The door of a furnace to a boiler.

Fire eater.—An old term for a rapid setter of type.

Firing.—A press or machine is said to be " firing " when friction is caused from want of lubrication.

*First.—The senior or leading partner of the two men who work at a hand-press.

*First forme.—The inner or outer of a forme—whichever is printed off first.

*First page.—The outside or first page of any printed sheet—that which contains the signature.

First proof.—The first pull of a forme after composing, which is read for the first time by the copy. See " Foul proof."

Fist.—A slang expression for an index mark, thus ☞ sometimes called " mutton-fist."

Five-em spaces.—" Thin " spaces, cast five to the em of any particular body.

Flat.—An expression used to indicate excessive flatness in an illustration owing to want of light and shade in overlaying.

Flat paper.—Paper sent in in reams not folded or quired.

Flat pull (or **impression**).—A simple proof without under or overlaying.

Flexible.—A term used in giving directions to a binder for sewing or binding in that style.

Flies.—Automatic takers-off on a machine; sometimes called " flyers."

Flimsy.—Thin paper, such as bank paper, telegraph forms, etc., is thus termed in printers' slang.

Flong.—The prepared paper used for making the moulds for casting stereo by the paper process.

*Flowers.—Floral ornaments used for borders, etc.

Fly.—The taker-off on a machine is sometimes thus termed.

*Fly.—Printer's devils were sometimes thus called.

Flyleaf.—A blank leaf not printed on.

Fly-title.—The half-title in front of the general title, or which divides sections of a work.

Fly-wheel.—A wheel which gives impetus to an engine or machine.

Flyers.—Taking-off apparatus attached to a printing machine.

Flying a frisket.—The process of turning up or down the tympan when printing at a hand-press.

*Folio.—A sheet of paper folded in two leaves only.

Fol.—Abbreviation for the word "folio" frequently used by booksellers in their catalogues.

Folio chase.—A chase with one bar only.

*Folios.—This term is applied to the enumeration of pages.

Folded paper.—Paper which is done up in reams folded in half, or quired—not flat.

Folder.—The bone implement used for folding in the warehouse.

Folders.—The hands in a warehouse who do the folding.

Folding chases.—Chases made in pairs or quadruple for facilitating the printing of large sheets, such as newspapers, on a machine.

Folding stick.—The bone stick used in folding.   See "Folder."

*Follow.—To see that sheets in a gathered book are in sequence.   Also used in other departments—by a compositor to see that copy "follows," or a pressman in perfecting to see that his folios "follow."

Followers.—The following sheets after a heading—such as the ordinary plain-ruled paper used after the title-head of a long invoice.

Foolscap.—A size of printing paper, 17 × 13½ inches; writing paper, 16¾ × 13½ inches.

*Foot of a letter.—The bottom of the shank of a type; usually grooved to prevent it wearing round.

*Foot of the page.—The bottom portion of a page.

*Footline.—The bottom line in a page.

*Footstep.—The inclined footstool the pressman puts his foot on when pulling the bar over.

*Footstick.—A bevelled stick put at the bottom of a page or pages to quoin up against. See " Sidestick."

Fore-edge.—The outer side edge of a book, distinct from head or tail, when folded.

Forestay of press.—The leg which supports the frame or ribs of a hand-press.

Forks.—Receptacles which hold the spindles of machine rollers.

Forme (or ***form**).—Pages of type when imposed in a chase constitute a " forme."

Forme carriage.—A small trolley on two wheels for moving formes about.

Forme gauge.—Gauge used for measuring margins of formes.

Forme hook.—A hook used for fishing small formes out of the lye trough.

Forme lift.—A lift to carry formes from floor to floor.

Forme racks.—Racks made for holding formes in a perpendicular position.

Forme trolley.—See " Forme carriage."

Fortnight.—A familiar term amongst printers to express notice to leave a situation—a fortnight's notice being the recognized custom on either side.

Forty-eightmo.—A sheet of paper folded into forty-eight leaves—written shortly, 48mo.

Fortymo.—A sheet of paper folded into forty leaves—written shortly, 40mo.

*Foul proof.—A proof distinct from a clean proof.

Foul stone.—If type or tools are left on the stone or imposing surface. See " Clear the stone."

*Founder.—Short term for the letter or type-founder.

Foundry chases.—Small chases used for imposing pages in convenient quantities for stereotyping or ēlectrotyping.

Foundry clumps.—Pieces of metal type-high placed round pages chiefly to form the bevel of the plate when cast.

Foundry proof.—The final proof before stereotyping or electrotyping which is generally supplied to the foundry.

*Fount.—This term is applied to the whole number of letters constituting a complete fount of any particular class of face or body.

Fount case rack.—Large racks made specially for holding these cases in.

Fount cases.—Cases of a larger kind than usual, for holding surplus sorts.

*Fount of letter.—A complete fount of type consists of capitals, small capitals, lower-case, figures, accents, points, spaces, etc.

Fount of type.—See " Fount of letter."

Four-em braces.—Braces cast on four ems of any particular body.

Four-em quads.—Large quadrats cast to four ems of any particular body.

Four-em spaces.—" Middling " spaces, cast four to the em of any particular body.

Four on.—An expression used in jobbing work where the job is printed quadruple to economize working.

Four set.—See " Four on."

Fours.—A familiar term used by compositors for " quarto."

Fourteen-to-pica leads.—Very thin leads cast fourteen to a pica.

Four to pica brass.—Brass rule made four to a pica in thickness.

Four to pica leads.—Leads cast four to a pica—generally called " thick leads."

Foxed.—Paper or books stained or mouldy are said to be "foxed."

F. p.—Abbreviation for " fine paper," that is, a better edition.

Fractions.—Fractional figures cast on single types. They are sometimes cast on half bodies, and then called "split fractions."

Fractur.—German expression for their text or black letter characters.

Fragments.—The odd pages at the commencement and end of a work—now usually called "oddments."

*****Frame.**—The wooden stand on which cases are placed to compose from, and usually made with racks in which to place cases.

Frame bed.—The shelf at the lower portion of the frame.

Frame drawer.—A drawer attached to the frame to hold copy, etc.

Frame rack.—A rack attached to the frame for cases not in immediate use.

Franklin press.—An American small jobbing platen machine.

French metal blocks.—The metal mounting cores or risers used for stereotype plates.

French metal furniture.—Metal furniture used in place of wooden—originally a French idea.

French pins.—Small wire nails or brads used for fastening plates to blocks.

French rules.—Short ornamental rules of either brass or type metal are generally thus designated.

French stereo blocks.—See "French metal blocks."

French type.—The nicks on these founts are placed on the back instead of the front.

Frenchman.—A perfecting machine originally of French make, but improved by English manufacturers, and now called Anglo-French machine.

Fresh paragraph.—To begin a fresh sentence at the commencement of a line by indentation.

Fresh rollers.—Rollers when too new are said to be "fresh."

Fret.—When rollers crack or peel they are said to " fret."

*Friar.—A light or broken patch in a printed sheet.

*Frisket.—A thin iron frame joined to the tympan. Its object is to prevent the sheet being dirtied or blackened, by pasting a sheet over the frame and cutting out only the parts to be printed.

Frisket button.—A button on the sides of the tympan.

*Frisket joints.—The parts which connect, usually with a pin, the frisket to the tympan.

*Frisket pins.—The pins which fasten the frisket to the tympan.

*Frisket stay.—A wooden stop fastened to the ceiling to prevent the frisket flying too far back.

Front marks.—The lay marks on the board nearest the grippers.

Frontispiece.—The illustration facing the title-page of a work.

*Frozen out.—An old term used when the workmen were hindered working through extreme cold. This is now obviated by warming the offices with steam or hot water.

Fudge.—To make shift with anything—a botch.

Fugitive colours.—A class of coloured inks which are not permanent in tone, and change or fade on exposure.

Full bound.—A term sometimes used to define a book wholly bound in leather.

*Full case.—A case well filled with type.

Full colour.—When ample ink has been used in printing.

Full-faced letter.—A fount of capitals which has no beard on the top of the shank, occupying the whole depth of the body.

*Full forme.—A forme distinct from a " broken," or one with blank pages in.

E

Full frame.—A compositor in a regular situation is said to have a " full frame."

Full measure.—Type composed the full width, and not in half measure or columns.

*****Full page.**—A page distinct from a short one.

Full point.—Technical name for a period or " full stop "—a mark of punctuation.

Full.—Short term used in the reading department for " full-point" or " full-stop."

*****Full press.**—When two men work at a press as partners.

Full stop.—A mark of punctuation, technically called a " full point."

*****Furniture.**—The wood used in making margin for a printed sheet, the thinner kind being usually called " Reglet." Sometimes French metal furniture is used.

Furniture (Sizes of).—Double broad, double narrow, broad, narrow, etc.

Furniture gauge.—The gauge used in measuring the furniture of a forme before sending it to press.

G

Is the sixth signature of the printer's alphabet.

ALLEY.*—These are wooden or zinc receptacles for holding type before making-up into pages.

Galley press.—A small hand-press for pulling proofs in slip form—sometimes of cylindrical make.

Galley rack.—Receptacles for galleys.

*Galley slaves.—An old term applied to compositors—the reason being obvious.

Galley sticks.—Long side-sticks used for quoining up galleys.

*Gallows.—A frame used for supporting the tympans of the old wooden presses when turned up.

*Garter of press.—A part of the old wooden press used in connection with the bar-handle in raising the platen after an impression was taken.

Gas engine.—A motor propelled by gas of different man or horse powers.

Gather corrections.—For facilitating corrections in a forme, compositors collect in their fingers the various and necessary letters required for the alterations.

*Gathering.—When a volume is wholly printed off, the sheets after drying and pressing are gathered in single copies of complete books; in half-sheet work there would be two copies on.

Gathering table.—A table, usually arranged horse-shoe shape, where the different sheets of a volume are laid down for gathering into books. Circular revolving tables are some-times used, the gatherer standing in one position and taking a sheet off as the table revolves.

Gauge.—A gauge to regulate length of page or margins. See "Page gauge," and "Furniture gauge."

Gauge glasses.—The glass tubes on the front of boilers to indicate the height of the water in the boiler.

Gem.—A size of type one size larger than Brilliant and one size smaller than Diamond.

Gentlemen's card.—A size of card, 3 × 1½ inches. Also called "thirds" (a third of a "large" card).

Geometrical signs.—Special characters relating to geometry.

German.—The particular character of type—somewhat similar to black letter—used for composing books in the German language. See "Fractur."

German cases.—These are cases of a special lay for founts used in composing this language.

German-silver sticks.—Composing sticks are sometimes made of this alloy.

Get in.—To set matter closely spaced.

*Gets in.—A term used when matter makes less than antici-. pated.

Get up.—This is an expression used as an order, *i.e.* to "get up" or compose certain copy.

G. H.—Is a printer's slang term to express his previous know-ledge of a fact.

G. I.—A printer's slang expression for "general indulgence," such as celebrating a birthday or an apprentice "coming out of his time."

Gill's machine.—A hot-rolling machine much used at the present time for drying and pressing work as it is printed off—thus greatly expediting delivery.

Gilt edges.—Books or cards with gilded edges are thus described.

Gilt tops.—Books usually on hand-made paper are sometimes bound with the top edges cut and gilt, thus preventing them being soiled by the dust that would otherwise collect if they were left rough.

*Girth wheel.—The drum on which the girthing winds in the running in or out of the press carriage.

*Girthing.—A kind of webbing regulating the running in and out of the carriage of a press.

Glazed boards.—Millboards, very hard and highly rolled, used for pressing printed sheets in the warehouse.

Gloss inks.—Inks of various colours having a very glossy appearance when dry.

G. M.—A slang abbreviation for " general manager " of a printing office.

Gods.—The nine quadrats used in throwing or "jeffing" by compositors.

Gold bronze.—Very fine powder used in gold-printing. It is dusted on after the forme is printed with a preparation specially made for the purpose.

Gold edges.—Another term for " Gilt edges," which see.

Gold leaf.—Gold beaten into very thin leaves—occasionally used for printing purposes, but more particularly for the decoration of book covers.

Gold printing.—In letterpress printing any work executed in gold by the bronze process.

Good colour.—When the ink is properly applied to a sheet —neither too much nor too little—but of a good and even depth.

*Good copy.—Plain, legible, and straightforward MS. or reprint. Applied to " fat " copy also.

Good matter.—Composed type not printed, or ordered to be kept standing with a view to reprinting.

*Good of the chapel.—Fines and dues which are collected for the chapel fund—to be disbursed as voted by the chapel.

'Goose.—Printers' abbreviation for " wayzgoose," or beanfeast.

Gordon press.—A small treadle platen machine made by Messrs. Powell and Son.

Got up.—An expression used to indicate that type is all used or copy is all composed.

Gothic.—An antique character of type similar to black letter.

Governor.—A synonym for the master or head of the establishment.

Governor of engine.—The two balls on an engine which check the supply of steam to the cylinder.

Grammar matter.—This is a class of composition paid for by a particular scale of prices.

'Graph processes.—The different kinds of printing from a transfer laid on gelatine or glue, such as the "papyrograph."

Graphic machine.—A single cylinder machine so named because first used for the " Graphic " newspaper.

Grass hand.—A compositor temporarily engaged—a practice common in newspaper offices.

Grassing.—A compositor taking occasional jobs, or assisting on a newspaper.

*Grave accent.—A sign over a letter, thus à

Grease.—A slang expression for the more technical one of " fat," *i.e.* good work.

*Great numbers.—Long working numbers in printing were thus called.

*Great Primer.—A size of type one size larger than English and one size smaller than Paragon, equalling two Bourgeois.

Great Primer reglet.—Wooden furniture of that depth in body.

*Greek.—The particular character of type used for works in the Greek language.

Greek cases.—These are cases of special lay for composing works in that language—the upper case being especially complicated by reason of the many accents required.

Gripper.—The fingers which grip a sheet in printing on a machine.

Gripper machines.—Machines which use fingers or grippers for laying on the sheets, in contradistinction to machines with other contrivances for laying on, such as the "Web."

Groove.—The groove in the short bar of a chase to allow of the pointing of a sheet at press.

Guard.—The fence or railing round a dangerous piece of machinery.

Guard.—A narrow strip sewn or turned in in a book for mounting plates or maps on.

Guarded.—Books are said to be "guarded" when the plates are mounted or sewn on guards instead of being stitched or pasted in the ordinary way.

Guillotine cutting machine.—A machine made for cutting paper on the "Guillotine" principle.

Gull.—If points are blunt or thick and tear the point-hole on the sheet, they are said to be "gulled."

Gummed paper.—Paper in various colours or sizes ready gummed is sold by most stationers.

Gun-metal shooting stick.—Locking-up sticks are sometimes tipped with gun-metal to render them more durable.

Gutter.—The "back" margin or furniture of a sheet. This is the part of a sheet which when folded falls in the back of the book.

***Gutter sticks.**—An old term for the back or gutter furniture.

H

Is the seventh signature of the printer's alphabet.

AIR leads.—Very thin leads—mostly sixteen to a pica—rarely used nowadays.

Hair-line letter. — Very thin-faced type, generally used for letterings of mounts.

Hair spaces.—Very thin spaces, used mostly for spacing out the letters in headlines of pages.

Half bound.—Books partly bound in leather, with cloth or paper sides.

Half cases.—Small cases used for jobbing purposes.

Half frame.—Small composing frames made to hold one pair of cases only.

Half large cards.—A size of card, 3 × 2¼ inches.

Half plate paper.—Machine-made paper of fine and soft texture used for woodcuts.

*Half press.—When instead of two one man only is working at a press.

*Half-sheet.—Book-work is sometimes printed in "half-sheet" fashion. When thus printed there are two copies on one sheet.

Half tints.—A term applied to the parts of an illustration of partial depth.

Half-title.—The sub-title in front of the full title.

*Hammer.—The tool used by pressmen or machine-minders for locking-up the formes on the bed or coffin.

Hammering.—A slang term used to express the overcharging of work done, especially when on time work.

Hand.—This term is applied to press work in contradistinction to machine work.

Handbills.—A common class of jobbing work which comprises circulars or letters.

*Handle.—Applied to both the " bar " and " rounce," handle.

Hand-made paper.—Paper made entirely by hand—a slow and tedious process—used chiefly for éditions de luxe.

Hand-made reams.—These generally run 480 sheets to a ream—occasionally 500, or even 516.

Hand roller.—Applied to the press roller used by machine-minders in pulling a proof to obviate running up colour with the machine rollers.

Hang it out.—A slang expression used by printers to denote skulking.

Hang off.—A slang term sometimes used by printers to express avoidance or indifference.

Hang up.—To hang printed work upon poles for drying.

Hanger.—An iron bracket attached to the ceiling to hold shafting.

Hanging galley.—A small galley with hooks to hang on the upper case.

*Hangs.—Type is said to hang when it is not squarely locked-up and the corners droop. It is also caused by pages being improperly gauged.

Hard impression.—Too much "pull" on the forme, but sometimes necessary for certain classes of work by reason of paper, etc.

Hard ink.—Ink when too much boiled is thus designated.

Hard packing.—An American system of making ready for printing dry paper.

Hard paper.—Paper of hard texture, different from plate paper or "soft" paper.

*Hard pull.—When the bar of the press goes stiffly it is said to be a hard pull.

Hard sized paper.—Paper more than ordinarily sized—writing papers are thus made.

Hatton machine.—A small treadle platen machine made by Messrs. J. Richmond and Co.

Haven cap.—A size of brown paper, 26 × 21 inches.

*Head.—The top part of a press, or the top part of a page.

*Headline.—The top line or heading of the page which runs throughout the book.

Head page.—The first or "dropped" page of a book, or a chapter or section thereof.

Headpieces.—Ornamental headings to pages, placed at the commencement of a book or chapter.

Head rule.—The rule sometimes used after a headline.

Heading chases.—Oblong chases used for imposing the headings of account books, etc.

Heads.—A term applied to the margin of books at the top of the page.

*Headsticks.—An old term for the head furniture.

*Heap.—A working or pile of paper, printed or not printed.

*Hebrew.—The particular character of type used for composing books in that language.

Hebrew cases.—Cases of special lay used for composing books in that language.

*Height to paper.—A general expression to denote the height of type. French type is slightly higher than English, consequently its "height to paper" is greater. Worn type is "low to paper."

Hell box.—A receptacle for battered or broken letters—in olden times a boot was used.

Herculean rule cutter.—A small but very strong cutting machine for rules or leads.

*****High.**—Type or blocks which stand higher than the rest of the forme. New type would stand higher than that worn.

High quadrats.—See " High spaces."

High spaces.—Spaces specially cast nearly type-high. They are used in plaster stereotyping mostly for cleanliness.

*****Hind parts of press.**—The supports at the end of the ribs which hold that part up.

*****Hither cheek.**—The side of the cheek which is nearest the pressman as he works.

Hoarding sorts.—To hide any particular or scarce letter of a fount in use.

Hoe machines.—Machines of various patterns made by Messrs. Hoe and Co. of New York.

Hoe platen machine.—A machine made by Messrs. Hoe and Co. of New York.

*****Holds out.**—A term used if paper or type is of ample quantity.

*****Hole.**—An ancient term for a private or unlicensed printing office.

Holyrood paper.—A particular kind of laid writing paper.

Hook down.—The end of a line turned over, and bracketed in the line below.

Hook in.—In almanack matter, etc., when the words are too many to come into the line they are hooked up or down.

Hook up.—The end of a line turned over, and bracketed in the line above.

Horizontal engine.—A motor the reverse of a vertical one.

Hornbeam.—A very hard wood used for bearers, etc.

*****Horse.**—An inclined stage set on the bank to hold the heap which has to be printed.

*Horse.—A slang expression for charging on account of work in hand but not finished.

*Horseflesh.—An old expression for the more modern one of " horse," which see.

Horse-power.—The driving power of engines is determined by horse-power.

*Horses.—Pressmen were thus called, on account of the arduous and exhausting character of their labour.

Hot pressing.—A mode of pressing by means of hot plates laid at intervals between the ordinary pressing boards, and placed in a powerful press.

Hot rolling.—A mode of rolling by means of heated rollers which both dry and press the work at the same time.

Hours.—Compositors reckon their lines when working in companionships by " hours," according to the size of the type and its measure.

*Hours.—Pressmen count their work in tokens of 250 pulls as " hours."

House.—A term applied to a firm or establishment.   See " The house."

House marks.—Corrections in proofs which the piece-hand is not expected to execute.

Hundred and twenty-eightmo.—Book-work of a small size—any sheet that could be folded into 128 leaves—written shortly, 128mo.

Hydraulic press.—Presses in which the power is applied by means of water pressure.

Hyphen.—A mark [-] used for dividing words at the end of a line, or for compounding words.

I

Is the eighth signature of the printer's alphabet.

MITATION parchment.—Paper chemically treated so as to resemble parchment.

Imitation vellum.—A prepared paper made to resemble vellum; made from the Japanese vellum paper.

Imperfect paper.—Reams of paper not made up to the full number of a printer's ream, *i.e.* 516 sheets. Hand-made, drawing, and writing papers are generally imperfect, and run 472, 480, or 500 sheets to the ream.

*Imperfections.—Short sorts required to perfect a type-founder's bill for a fount of a certain weight.

*Imperfections.—Sheets required by a binder to make good books imperfect through bad gathering, collating, or spoiled sheets.

Imperial.—A size of printing paper, 30 × 22 inches; writing paper, 34 × 22 inches.

Imperial cap.—A size of brown paper, 29 × 22 inches.

Imperial press.—A hand-press between a Stanhope and an Albion invented by Messrs. Sherwin and Cope many years ago.

*Imposing stone.—A perfectly smooth stone or iron surface on which formes are imposed and corrected, embedded in a strong wooden frame on legs, if stone; if iron, laid on the frame.

Imposing surface.—Another term for "imposing stone," which see.

*Imposition.—The art of laying pages down so that when printed they fall correctly in folding.

Imposition book.—The book used in the composing-room to indicate the progress of a work and the number of pages credited to each compositor.

Imposition scales.—The various schemes or plans by which pages are laid down on the stone for imposition.

Imposition schemes.—See " Imposition scales."

*Impression.—The pressure applied to the forme by means of a platen or cylinder to give a print from type.

Impression screws.—The screws which regulate the amount of pressure in a printing press or machine.

Impression sheets.—The sheets which are placed between the tympan or round the cylinder to receive the impression.

Imprint.—By an old act of parliament a printer is required to affix his name and address to a work (with certain exceptions), and this is termed an imprint.

In boards.—A general term used to indicate that books are bound in boards, in contradistinction to paper wrappers.

In bulk.—A general term applied to large quantities—the reverse of anything usually packed or " done up " in small quantities.

In chase.—Type imposed, as distinguished from that on galley or packed away in the store-room.

In cloth.—Books bound in cloth, in contradistinction to those in paper covers or bound in leather.

In forme.—Type made up and imposed.   See " In chase."

In galley.—Matter pulled in slips instead of being made up into pages and imposed.

In leather.—Bound books are thus described, to distinguish them from those in paper covers or bound in cloth.

*In pages.—All the pages of a sheet other than the first or outer page.

In pages.—Matter made up into pages before pulling proof—the reverse of proof in slip.

In paper.—Books or pamphlets folded and sewn in paper covers.

In press.—Sheets being cold pressed are said to be "in press."

In quires.—Books in sheets not bound up.

In sheets.—Books not bound, but in quires.

In slip.—Matter set up and pulled on galleys before making-up into pages.

In the hole.—A compositor behindhand with his copy, and keeping his companions waiting, is thus described.

In the metal.—Anything in type—the reverse of anything in print; for instance, to read a revise "in the metal" before taking a proof.

In the opening.—When compositors await a companion finishing his copy in order that the making-up may be passed, the person so waited for is said to be "in the opening."

In the press.—A work in course of printing is thus announced to the trade or public.

In type.—Matter yet standing—not cleared away or broken up.

In use.—Obviously any fount of type, or cases for same, when engaged.

Incut notes.—Side-notes which are let into the text, instead of being in the margin.

Indelible ink.—Special inks so made; used mostly for marking inks.

*****Indent.**—A line set back a little; for instance, the commencement of a paragraph, which is generally indented an em.

Index.—The sign of a hand or fist ☞ Also the reference index at the end of a work.

Index matter.—Matter pertaining to the index at the end of a work.

India paper.—A fine paper used by engravers for proofs, which, though generally imported from China, is called "India."

India proofs.—Artists' or engravers' proofs pulled on India paper.

India rubbered.—Books when interspersed with plates are sometimes coated at the back with india rubber to save stitching or expense of guarding—when open the book will lie perfectly flat.

India-rubber blanket.—Blankets made of this material are useful for bringing up type when partly worn—a hard impression being best for new type.

Indorse.—The titles of legal documents or prospectuses, which appear on the outside when folded up. See "Endorse."

Inferior figures.—Special figures cast or made to range at the bottom of a letter, thus—$_{1\,2\,3}$

Inferior letters.—Small letters which are cast on the lower part of the body, *e.g.* $_{a\ e\ i\ o\ u}$—the reverse of "superior" letters—$^{a\ e\ i\ o\ u}$

Ingram machine.—A rotary machine named after the late proprietor of the "Illustrated London News."

Initial letters.—Large block or floriated letters used at the commencement of a chapter or work.

*****Ink.**—The pigment of various colours which imparts the print to a sheet on impression being applied to type.

*****Ink block.**—The board on which the ink was distributed for the old ink-balls.

*****Ink brayer.**—A small wooden implement for rubbing out the ink on the table.

Ink cylinder.—The revolving iron roller in the ink ductor which imparts a given quantity of ink to the vibrating roller.

Ink ductor.—The receptacle similar to a trough which holds the ink at the end of a machine.

Ink fountain.—The ductor of a machine is sometimes thus called.

Ink knife.—The long blade in the ductor which regulates by means of keys the amount of ink to be given at each impression.

*****Ink muller.**—A wooden implement used for rubbing out the ink on the table.

Ink slab.—The table on which ink is distributed, either at press or machine.

*****Ink slice.**—A small iron implement used for lifting ink out of cans.

Ink solvent.—A wash for cleansing type.

Ink table.—The surface on which ink is distributed.

Ink up.—To run up colour on the rollers, or to coat press rollers with a coarse preservative ink when out of use.

Inkers.—The large rollers on the printing machine which apply the ink to the type.

Inking apparatus.—The parts of a machine applied for inking purposes.

Inkoleum.—An American patent liquid used with ink for thinning purposes or to facilitate drying.

Inner forme.—The pages of type which fall on the inside of a printed sheet in "sheet" work—the reverse of "outer" forme.

*****Inner tympan.**—The reverse of the "outer" tympan—the side which is lifted to place the sheets in.

Insensible ink.—An ink which cannot be tampered with or effaced by chemicals.

*****Insertion.**—Copy left out by accident, or additional words or copy supplied by an author, is thus termed.

Inset.—A sheet, or part of a sheet, to be placed inside another sheet to complete sequence of pagination.

F

*Inside quires.—The good quires of a ream—distinct from "outsides."

Inside reams.—Good and selected paper—applied more especially to drawing or hand-made papers—of 480 sheets; mill reams of 472 sheets contain top and bottom "outside" quires.

Intaglio.—Printing, such as from copperplate—the reverse of "relief" printing.

Interleaved.—When woodcuts are printed they are usually sheeted to prevent set-off. Bookbinders also place thin paper in front of plates in binding with the same object.

Interleaves.—Separate leaves of descriptive matter cut up and interleaved between the plates of an illustrated work.

Interlinear matter.—Small type between lines of larger character.

Interrogation.—A mark or note of interrogation (?) sometimes used as a query by readers.

Inter.—Abbreviation used in the reading department for "note of interrogation."

Interrogatories.—A class of legal work—questions and answers.

Introduction.—A term applied to the preliminary or introductory portion of a work.

Inverted commas.—Extract matter or names of works are placed between inverted commas, thus "and"

Invictus machine.—A small treadle platen machine used for jobbing purposes.

Irish.—The character of type used to compose works in that language.

Irish cases.—A particular kind of cases, with a special lay, for composing works in that language.

Iron composing stick.—The tool mostly used by compositors, though sticks are sometimes made of wood, gun-metal, and German silver.

Iron shooter.—Special sticks made for locking up formes where the quoins are small.

*Italic.—The sloping characters—distinct from roman types—invented by *Aldus Manutius, a Venetian printer.*

*Italic cases.—Cases—as distinguished from roman ones—for holding italic founts.

Italicised.—Words or sentences in italic—indicated in MS. by a single line underneath.

Its own body.—This term is applied to the text type of a work to distinguish it from the note or appendix types, usually smaller.

Its own paper.—The particular kind of paper used for a certain work—a proof is sometimes asked for on "its own paper."

J

Is not used as a signature in the printer's alphabet.

**ACKET.**—A movable border round a letter or initial.

Japanese paper.—Very thin paper of a silky texture made in Japan and used for artists' proofs, etc.

Japanese vellum paper.—Thick hand-made paper with a vellum surface manufactured in Japan.

Jeff.—To throw or gamble with quadrats as with dice.

Jemmy.—An implement with a flattened toe for raising formes in lifting off the press.

Jerry.—The noise made by beating chases, etc., on an apprentice finishing his time.

Jigger.—A small box with divisions to hold peculiar sorts, usually made of quadrats and leads.

Job.—Any work which makes less than a sheet.

Job chases.—Small chases used for jobbing purposes.

Job fount.—A small fount of type used for displaying purposes—distinct from a book fount.

Job house.—A term applied to printing offices distinct from book or newspaper offices.

Jobbing cases.—Double cases made with upper and lower in one. They are sometimes made treble.

Jobbing galleys.—Galleys of various sizes and widths suitable for miscellaneous work.

Jobbing machines.—The small treadle platen machines.

Jobbing stick.—Composing stick with lever attachment for facilitating the changing of measures.

Join up.—To bring two or more corners close together in a border; also the " closing-up " of two consecutive takes of copy.

*Justification.—This term is applied generally to the even and equal spacing of words and lines to a given measure.

Justifiers.—Another term for quotations or quadrats.

*Justify.—To space out to any given measure.

*Justifying a stick.—To make a stick up to a given measure.

K

Is the ninth signature of the printer's alphabet.

. D.—A slang expression sometimes used by printers—to "keep dark."

Keep down.—An instruction to use capital letters somewhat sparingly.

*Keep in.—To set type closely spaced. See "Get in."

*Keep out.—To set type widely spaced. See "Drive out."

Keep standing.—Type kept in abeyance pending possibility of reprint.

Keep up.—An instruction to use capitals somewhat freely; also to keep type standing.

Kent cap.—A size of brown paper, 21 × 19 inches.

*Kern.—The under part of any letter which overhangs the shank or body, as in some italic founts.

Key.—The wedge which tightens a wheel on the shaft of a machine.

Kidder press.—An American small rotary jobbing machine.

King's paper.—A particular kind of hand-made paper manufactured at the mill established by the maker of that name.

Kiss.—When rollers on a machine fret against each other they are said to "kiss."

Knib of setting rule.—The nose of the rule which the compositor lifts up line by line as the type is composed.

Knock off.—A somewhat slangy term used by printers occasionally to express leaving off work for meals or for the day.

*Knock up.—To make the edges of a heap of paper straight and square by knocking up to one edge.

Koenig machine.—The first printing machine was designed by Friedrich Koenig, a German.

L

Is the tenth signature of the printer's alphabet.

**ABEL punches.**—Sharp steel dies of various shapes for cutting labels in quantities.

Labels.—The class of work which comes under this category—address, parcel, luggage, etc. labels.

Laces.—The leather laces which fasten the ends of bands or straps together.

Ladies' cards.—The particular cards used for this purpose are "smalls," size $3\frac{1}{2} \times 2\frac{1}{2}$ inches.

Laid paper.—Paper showing the wire or dandy marks.

Laid up.—When a forme is printed off and required for distribution, it is said to be "laid-up" when washed, placed on the board, and unlocked. The same term is applied to a forme placed on the imposing surface and ready for correction.

Lapped paper.—Reams of paper sent in flat, *i.e.* not folded, with the two ends lapped over—thus being divided into three.

Large cards.—A size of card, $4\frac{1}{2} \times 3$ inches.

Large court envelopes.—To take large post 8vo in half, $5\frac{1}{2} \times 4\frac{1}{4}$ inches.

Large post.—A size of writing paper, $21 \times 16\frac{1}{2}$ inches.

*Latin.—The class of work composed in that language.

Latin type.—A fancy character of letter for display work.

Law work.—A general term for legal work of any kind.

Lay.—This refers to the position of the print on a sheet of paper.

Lay down.—To put pages on the stone for imposition.

Lay marks.—The marks or stops used for laying the sheet to in printing.

*Lay on.—To feed or lay on the sheets one by one in printing.

Lay on forme.—To put a forme on the press or machine for printing.

Lay on press.—An instruction to put a forme on the press preparatory to printing.

Lay type.—To put new sorts in cases.

Layer on.—The feeder on a printing machine.

Laying letter.—The putting of new type into cases is thus termed.

Laying-on board.—The board on which the " white " paper is laid, and from which it is fed sheet by sheet.

Laying-up board.—The wooden board on which formes are laid up for distribution.

*Lean.—Close and poor work for piece-hands.

*Lean face.—A thin or meagre-faced fount of letter. The reverse of " fat face."

Lead box.—The receptacle for broken or small pieces of leads.

Lead case.—Special cases or trays for holding leads in their respective sizes and thicknesses.

Lead cutter.—A machine for the cutting of leads or brass rule.

Lead galley.—A galley for holding leads of various sizes and kinds for jobbing purposes.

Lead moulds.—The apparatus for casting leads in lengths, which are afterwards cut to sizes.

Lead out.—To white or spread out by means of leads.

Lead racks.—Receptacles for holding assorted leads.

Leaded matter.—Type with leads between the lines—in contradistinction to " solid " matter.

Leaders.—Dots or full points cast on an em of any particular body, thus ...

Leads.—Strips of lead cast to different thicknesses and cut to various sizes.

Leads (Sizes of).—Thick (four to pica), thin (eight to pica), six, ten, twelve, fourteen, and sixteen to pica in thickness.

Leaflets.—Jobs printed on single leaves, either one or both sides.

Leatherette.—An imitation of leather—usually made of embossed paper.

Leatheroid.—An imitation leather made of cloth or paper.

Left-hand pages.—Those pages which fall on the left-hand side of a book and have even folios.

Legal work.—The general term for law work of any kind.

Let-in notes.—Another term for cut-in notes, *i.e.* let into the text, as distinct from side-notes.

*Letter.—A general term for type as a fount.

Letterals.—This term is applied to errors of single letters in proofs. See " Literals."

*Letter board.—Another term for laying-up boards, which see.

Letter brush.—A brush used for taking dust off type.

*Letter founders.—Otherwise type founders.

*Letter hangs.—When pages are not locked up squarely in the forme.

*Letter mould.—The apparatus used for hand casting of types.

Letter paper.—This term is applied to quarto paper—note paper being octavo.

Letterpress.—Printing from type as distinct from lithographic or plate printing.

Letter's out.—When type runs short through being all in use.

*Ley.—Another way of spelling "lye," the liquid used for cleansing type.

Liberty machine.—An American treadle platen machine for jobbing purposes.

Lift.—To raise a forme or type. Also applied to a handful of printed work in the warehouse.

Lift.—The apparatus for sending formes or paper from floor to floor.

Ligatures.—Two or more letters cast in one piece, such as ﬅ or ﬃ.

Light.—Slang term sometimes used by printers for giving or obtaining credit—applied more particularly to that obtained at public houses or beer-shops.

Light master.—An organizer or medium between lender and borrower, generally one of the men, who arranges such matters as payment, etc.

Light tints.—The lighter parts of an engraving in printing.

Lights.—See "Light tints."

Line book.—The book used by compositors in making up, showing the progress of any particular work, and the debtor and creditor account of lines to each hand engaged thereon.

Line is on.—When companionships of compositors have resumed work after an enforced idleness the line is said to be " on."

Line off.—In companionships of compositors it is customary to deduct a line off per hour to counterbalance the trouble of leading matter, etc.

*Line of quadrats.—A " white " line formed of quadrats.

Line of stars.—A line of asterisks, thus—

*   *   *   *   *   *

to indicate an omission in any sentence or paragraph.

Line on.—Sometimes a line on per hour is added when work is exceptionally fat.   See "Line off."

Lines.—A compositor on piece-work is said to be on his lines.

Linear papers.—Papers made with water-marked lines at given distances to guide handwriting.

Linen-faced paper.—Paper having one or both sides covered with linen. Folded cards are often linen-faced to prevent them breaking in half at the score.

Lining papers.—End or paste-down papers used by bookbinders.

Literals.—Another term for "letterals," errors of single letters in proofs.

Lithographic.—Pertaining to lithography.

Lithography.—The art of printing from stone.

Litho.—A general short term for lithography.

Lithophine.—An American preparation for preserving drawings and writing on stone.

Lithotint.—An etching process executed on lithographic stones.

Little Wonder.—A small jobbing platen machine, made by Messrs. Powell.

Live steam.—Good steam—the reverse of waste or exhaust steam.

LL.—The abbreviation used by booksellers to indicate the number of "leaves" in a book.

Loan paper.—A paper of hard, thin, and tough texture, used for documents and debenture forms.

*Lock-up.—To fasten up tightly the quoins of a forme by means of a mallet and shooting-stick.

Lock-up chases.—Special chases made in order to dispense with large quantities of furniture in filling up spare room in formes or on the press.

Lock-up iron.—The iron stick used for tightening up formes as they stand instead of laying them up.

Locking-up apparatus.—Applied to the various kinds of patent fastening, such as screws or iron wedges.

Logotypes.—Two or more letters, or sometimes words, cast in one piece.

London scale of prices.—The recognized scale of prices in vogue in London as agreed to by masters and men.

Long case rack.—Tall case racks distinct from frame racks.

*Long cross.—The longest cross-bar of a chase.

Long letters.—Accented letters used to denote contractions, pronunciation, as ā ē ī ō ū ñ p̄, etc.

Long measures.—Type composed in wide measures.

Long numbers.—Orders to print large numbers are thus called.

Long page.—A page of type which is a line longer than its companion pages.

*Long Primer.—A size of type one size larger than Bourgeois and one size smaller than Small Pica, equal to two Pearls.

Long Primer reglet.—Wooden furniture of that depth in body.

*Long pull.—When the bar-handle of a press is pulled right over.

Long s.—The old kind of " s " thus " ſ " used in old style or antique work.

Long takes.—Portions of copy given out to compositors in larger quantities than usual.

Long twelves.—A plan of imposition whereby the pages are laid down in two long rows of six pages.

Longs.—A general term for " long " accents.

*Loose justifying.—Lines badly spaced, *i.e.* not tight enough.

*Low.—When letters or other parts of a printed sheet do not show up clearly they are said to be " low."

*Low case.—When type is very nearly set out of a case.

Low quadrats.—Quadrats of ordinary height, as distinguished from the high quadrats formerly used for plaster stereo work.

Low spaces.—See " Low quadrats."

***Low to paper.**—Type when worn is of course lower than when new, and it is then said to be " low to paper."

Lower boards.—The under or taking-off boards on a printing machine.

***Lower case.**—The case which contains the small letters, points, and spaces—the lower of the pair of cases.

Lower case sorts.—Letters belonging to the lower case of the pair—distinct from capitals or small capitals.

L. p.—Abbreviation for " large paper " copies of works.

Lubricators.—Small glass globes placed on the shafting to lubricate the working parts of a machine.

Lug.—When rollers are tacky or stick together they are said to lug.

***Lye.**—The preparation used for cleansing type after printing.

***Lye brush.**—The article used in applying the liquid.

Lye jars.—Earthenware articles for storing lye.

***Lye trough.**—The receptacle for holding lye.

M

Is the eleventh signature of the printer's alphabet.

**ACHINE boys.**—The lads who lay on, take off, and job about generally in the machine department.

Machine men.—The workmen or "minders" who tend the machines.

Machine minder.—The skilled workman who is responsible for the care of the machine.

Machine paper.—Paper other than that made by hand.

Machine points.—Special points which are used in the machine department, and distinct from press points.

Machine rollers.—The various rollers in use for machine printing generally, such as inkers, vibrators, wavers, etc., which see respectively.

Machine room (or **department**).—That portion of a printing office occupied by the machines.

Machine tapes.—The narrow tapes which guide and carry the sheets from the cylinders in printing.

Machine work.—A general term for work executed by machine as distinct from hand-press.

Machines.—Mechanical appliances of various kinds, both platen and cylindrical, for printing purposes.

Machines (Varieties of).—Such as platen, cylinder, perfecting, rotary, jobbing, etc., which see respectively.

Mackle.—A printed sheet with a slurred appearance, owing to the frisket dragging, or a defect in the impression.

Macule.—See "Mackle."

Made-up.—When type is measured off into pages it is said to be made-up.

Magazines.—A class of periodical work which has a special and extra charge in composition.

Mag.—An abbreviation very generally used by printers for "magazine."

Main shafting.—The principal part of the shafting from which a number of machines are driven.

Main's machine.—A machine invented by Mr. T. Main, sometimes called a "tumbler" on account of its peculiar motion.

Make even.—In copy with long paragraphs, or in newspaper work, compositors have sometimes to finish their portions at the end of a line, in order to expedite the closing up of "takes." They are then said to "make even."

Make-up.—To measure off matter into pages.

Making margin.—To give the proper proportion of margin or furniture to a forme preparatory to imposition.

*Making measure.—To make the composing stick up to a given measure.

*Making ready.—Preparing for printing by patching up or cutting away, etc.

*Mallet.—A wooden hammer with a large head used for locking-up formes.

Maltese cross.—A religious sign, thus ✠

Man-hole.—The aperture in a boiler which admits of a person going inside for cleansing purposes.

Man power.—The power of the smaller engines, usually driven by gas, is determined by "man power." In the larger ones it is indicated by horse power.

Manifold paper.—Carbonized paper used largely by shop-keepers—especially drapers—for duplicating invoices.

Manilla paper.—Paper made of a fibre imported from Manilla.

Manuscript.—Written copy (MS.), which has a special scale in composition, distinct from "reprint" copy.

Map.—A slang expression for a proof on which there are a great number of marks.

Marbled edges.—The cut edges of books are often marbled instead of being gilt.

Marbled paper.—A particular kind of paper of various patterns generally used for end leaves and paste-downs of books.

*Margin.—The blank paper surrounding a page of print.

*Marginal notes.—Usually called side-notes ; sometimes in-cut, or let into the matter at the side.

Marinoni machine.—A French printing machine of rotary make, invented by a person of that name.

Mark.—This refers to the mark to which a sheet is laid in printing.

Marking ink.—Indelible ink used for marking linen, etc.

*Marks.—The corrections and alterations marked on a proof sheet.

Marks of reference.—Signs of various kinds used for notes, such as * † ‖ ¶ Sometimes superior figures or letters are so used.

Mary.—If none of the nicks appear uppermost in throwing or "jeffing" with quadrats, the throw is called a "Mary." See "Molly."

*Master printer.—The employer and head of a printing office.

Mathematical signs.—Various characters used in relation to mathematics.

*Matrice (or Matrix).—The copper mould with a punch struck in by which type is cast. Also called "Strikes."

*Matrices.—Plural of matrice or matrix.

*Matter.—Another term for composed type.

G

*Measure.—The given width of a page of type. Measures are generally made to pica ems, but sometimes in narrow or double-column matter an en is used in addition.

Medhurst's press.—An iron platen hand-press made in the early part of this century by Mr. Medhurst.

Medical contractions.—Abbreviated words used in medical works.

Medical signs.—Signs and characters appertaining to medicine.

Medium.—A size of printing paper, 19 × 24 inches ; writing, 22 × 17½ inches.

Melting kettle.—The utensil used for melting down composition for making rollers.

Melting pot.—See " Melting kettle."

*Metal.—The compound used for type or stereotype plates.

Metal furniture.—Furniture cast in an alloy of poorer quality than type metal.

Metal galley.—Galleys generally made of zinc, but sometimes of brass, used for newspaper work mostly.

Metal rule.—A general term for em rules or dashes. Also applied to longer rules, such as two, three, and four ems.

Metallic cards.—Cards made with a prepared enamelled surface.

Metallic quoins.—Patented iron quoins in lieu of the old wooden ones.

Miche (or **Mike**).—A printer's slang term for skulking or playing about.

Middling spaces.—Spaces cast four to an em of any particular body.

Millboard.—A species of board made very hard, and well rolled, used for the better class of bookbinding.

Milled.—Paper rolled or glazed—with a high surface.

Mill reams.—Hand-made paper only 472 sheets to a ream ; if all inside quires, 480.

Miller and Richard's type.—A term frequently used to describe the revived " old style " types initiated by the firm of that name.

Minders.—A short term very generally used for machine minders.

Minerva machine.—A small platen jobbing machine—the original " Cropper " machine.

Minion.—A size of type one size larger than Emerald and one size smaller than Brevier.

Minnikin.—A size of type smaller than Brilliant, and a fourth of Pica in body only.

Minute mark.—An accent mark (′) is used to express chronological or geographical minutes.

Minutes of evidence.—A class of legal work.

Miss.—An omission to lay a sheet on by the feeder of a machine.

Missing sheets.—Any omitted sheets from a gathered book.

Mitre.—To chamfer or bevel the ends of rules in order that they may join closely in forming a border.

Mitred corners.—Rules made with corners bevelled or chamfered.

Mitreing machine.—A mechanical appliance for chamfering or bevelling rules for borders, etc.

Mixture.—An extra charge involved on composition if three or more types are used in a work.

Model press.—A jobbing platen machine originally of American make, but now made in this country.

Modern-face type.—Founts of recent date, the reverse of antique or old-faced types.

Molly.—In throwing with quadrats if the nicks are not uppermost ; this reckons as a blank.   See " Mary."

*Monk.—A black patch on a printed sheet caused through insufficient distribution or bad ink.

Monkey wrench.—A screw hammer with an extending claw made to fit various sized nuts.

Monkeys.—Compositors were sometimes thus styled by pressmen in retaliation for being called by them "pigs."

Monotint.—Tint printing in any one colour.

'Mos.—A slang term frequently used by printers for "animosity."

Mottled cards.—Cards with a mottled surface of various colours.

Mottled paper.—Fancy paper made in various colours with mottled surfaces.

*Mould.—The apparatus for casting type—the matrix being placed inside.

Moulds.—Generally understood as the preliminary stage in stereotyping by paper process. Moulds of course are used for plaster work and electrotyping too.

Mounting wood.—The material, generally mahogany, on which stereotype or electrotype plates are mounted.

Mounts.—A class of printed work on which photographs, etc., are mounted.

Mouse roller.—A small additional roller for the better distribution of ink on a machine.

Movable.—A general term applied to type to distinguish it from stereotype, etc.

Movable bars.—Some chases are made with cross-bars which can be removed. This is sometimes a great convenience.

Movable cross-bars.—See "Movable bars."

M's and W's.—A slang expression used to define an intoxicated person's unsteady gait.

MS.—An abbreviation for manuscript.

MSS.—Plural of the abbreviation MS.—manuscripts.

Mucilage.—Any substance used for adhesive purposes.

*Muller.—A wooden implement used for rubbing out ink on the table or slab.

Multicolour letters.—Characters cut in separate pieces for working in two or more colours.

Multiple mark.—A sign in arithmetic, thus ×

Music cases.—Special cases of a complicated character for composing type-music.

Music demy.—A size of printing paper, $20\frac{3}{4} \times 14\frac{1}{8}$ inches.

Music of the press.—The noise occasioned in working a press in full swing is thus termed.

Music printing.—The art of printing music from type or plates.

Music type.—Special type used in letterpress printing distinct from engraved plates.

Mutton fist.—An index hand, thus  sometimes shortly called a "fist."

N

Is the twelfth signature of the printer's alphabet.

NAIL.—A printer's slang term for "backbiting" anyone.

Naked forme.—A forme of type waiting for— or stripped of—furniture.

Napier machine.—Platen machines made by Messrs. Napier.

Narrow.—Wooden furniture (sometimes of metal) three picas in width.

Narrow measures.—Type composed in narrow widths, as in column matter.

Near cheek.—The cheek nearest the pressmen.

Nearside of press.—The side of the press nearest the workman.

Neck of a letter.—The sloping part of a type from the shank to the face of the letter.

New paragraph.—The commencement of a section at a fresh line—usually indented an em.

N. P.—An abbreviation for "new paragraph," the commencement of a new line by means of indentation.

News composing stick.—These tools are often of mahogany lined with brass for the sake of lightness, and made up to a fixed measure.

News house.—Printing offices for that class of work—distinct from houses which lay themselves out for book-work and jobbing.

News quoins.—The larger kind of wooden quoins are thus termed, those used for book-work being of a smaller average.

News stick.—See " News composing stick."

Newspaper chases.—Specially made chases to allow of the pages being laid closely together on the machine. See "Folding chases."

N. F.—A slang term frequently used by printers—an abbreviation for " no fly," to feign ignorance or indifference.

Nicholson's machine.—This machine was devised by William Nicholson in the last century, and was the forerunner of all subsequent machines.

*Nick.—The groove or grooves placed in the shank of a letter to assist composition, and to discriminate between different founts.

Nickel face.—Electrotypes are often nickel-faced when they are to be used with red ink, as copper deteriorates the colour.

Night work.—Extra or late work charged as overtime.

Nippers.—A small implement used for correcting type—especially tabular work—instead of the ordinary bodkin.

Nipping press.—A small screw press for the more expeditious cold-pressing of jobs.

No return.—Another expression for the extra charge in composition for pamphlet—when a work is all got up without a return of type.

Noiseless forme carriage.—A small trolley with india-rubber tyred wheels.

*Nonpareil.—The size of a type one size larger than Pearl and one size smaller than Emerald—half of a Pica in depth of body.

Nonpareil brass rule.—Brass rules cast on this body are used for borders or column rules.

Nonpareil clumps.—Metal leads of that depth in body.

Nonpareil leads.—Leads cast to that depth in body.

Nonpareil reglet.—Wooden furniture of that depth in body.

Non-society hands.—Workmen distinct from those belonging to any trade organization.

Non-society houses.—Printing offices not recognizing the society scale or open to society hands.

Non-soc.—An abbreviation for " Non-society."

Northumbrian machine.—A rotary machine made for newspaper work.

Note of admiration.—A mark of punctuation, thus !

Note of exclamation.—The same as " note of admiration."

Note of interrogation.—A mark of punctuation, thus ?

Note papers.—These papers are octavo in shape, but of various sizes ; letter papers being quarto shape, and also of various sizes.

Note papers (Sizes of).—Large post, small post, Albert, Queen's, etc.

*****Notes.**—A general term for either marginal or foot-notes.

Numbering.—This is applied more particularly to the numbering or paging, double and otherwise, of cheque books, etc.

Numbering machine.—The mechanical appliance for numbering or paging purposes.

Numerals.—Numbering by means of Roman numerals, i, ii, iii, iv, etc., instead of Arabic figures, 1, 2, 3, etc.

O

Is the thirteenth signature of the printer's alphabet.

BELISK.—Usually called a "dagger," thus †
a mark of reference to foot-notes.

Oblong.—This is the reverse of "upright" in
speaking of any particular size—*i.e.* an "oblong"
8vo, not "upright" 8vo.

*Octavo.—A sheet of paper folded into eight—shortly written
thus—8vo.

Octavo points.—Long straight press-points, not elbowed as
"twelves" points.

Octodecimo.—A sheet folded into eighteen leaves.   See
"Eighteenmo," written shortly, 18mo.

Odd folios.—Those pages which fall on the right-hand side of
a book and are numbered 1, 3, 5, 7, etc.

*Odd pages.—See "Odd folios."

*Off.—When a press or machine has printed the required number
of copies, the forme is said to be "off."

Off cheek.—The cheek of the press on the farther side from
the workman.

Off colour.—A slang expression sometimes used by printers
to define a man neglecting his work, being out of condition.

Off-cut.—That part of the sheet which has to be cut off in
order that the sheet may be folded correctly, as in a "twelves."

Off its feet.—A term applied to type when it is not standing squarely on its feet.

*Off-set.—The set-off of ink from one sheet to another of printed work whilst wet.

Offside of press.—The side of the press farthest from the workman.

Official envelopes.—Long narrow envelopes, $8\frac{1}{4} \times 3\frac{3}{4}$ inches, to take fcap. folio when folded in four—used in official circles.

Oil can.—The utensil for holding oil for lubrication.

Oil holes.—Small apertures in various parts of a machine to allow of oil being readily applied in order to avoid friction.

Oiled paper.—Prepared paper for copying purposes. It is sometimes used for set-off sheets.

Old cut.—Anything pertaining to the old or antique style.

Old-cut type.—Founts similar to the Caslon old-faced type.

*Old English.—Founts of type of black-letter character.

O. E.—Abbreviation for the words Old English (black letter).

Old face.—See "Old cut."

Old-face type.—See "Old-cut type."

Old pelt.—An appellation for an old pressman in bygone days.

Old style.—See "Old cut" or "Old face."

Old-style type.—See "Old-cut type."

Old Turkey mill.—A machine writing paper of good quality.

O. T. M.—An abbreviation for "old Turkey mill" writing papers.

On galley.—Any type on galley—distinct from that made-up or paged.

On grass.—A compositor taking casual work is said to be "on grass." See "Smout."

On lines.—A compositor on piece-work is thus described.

On piece.—A printer engaged and paid by result of work done.

On the carpet.—A slang term sometimes used by printers when a workman is summoned before the authorities into the counting house.

On the gathering board.—Work in course of "gathering" into books is thus designated.

On time.—When a man is paid by the hour or week, and not by piece-work, he is said to be "on time."

On tramp.—Workmen on the road seeking employment from town to town.

One-sided machine.—Ordinary style of single cylinder machines.

O. P.—A publisher's term signifying that a book is "out of print."

*****Open matter.**—Fat and well-leaded work.

Open spacing.—Wide spacing between the words of a line or different lines.

*****Open the forme.**—To unloosen and open out the forme for cleansing purposes—or to unlock for correction.

*****Open work.**—Well leaded or otherwise "fat" matter.

Opening.—When a compositor has copy in hand unfinished, and the next man in order awaits the closing-up.

Organ.—In slang a man who lends money to his fellow-workmen at a weekly interest.

Otto gas engine.—A gas motor especially well adapted for driving printing machinery.

Ounce mark.—A medical sign, thus ℥

*****Out.**—An accidental omission of copy in composition.

Out of condition.—Printing rollers not in good order for working.

Out of copy.—When a compositor has finished his portion of copy, or the whole of the copy in hand is finished or is all given out by the clicker.

Out of his time.—An apprentice who has completed his indentured term is thus described.

Out of letter.—When type is scarce or all used up.

*****Out of register.**—When pages do not back one another line for line, or at head and foot, through bad gauging of pages or furniture.

Out of sorts.—When there is a run on any particular letter or letters, and these become scarce.

Out of type.—See " Out of letter."

Out of use.—When type or other material is standing by.

*****Out page.**—The first or signature page of a sheet.

Outer forme.—The outer side of a sheet of work.

*****Outer tympan.**—The larger tympan, into which the inner one fits.

Outside reams.—Reams of paper made up entirely of outside or damaged sheets.

*****Outsides.**—The top or bottom sheets of a ream—generally damaged and called " retree."

Ovals.—Borders or frames of that shape, generally made of brass.

Overcast.—A particular kind of book sewing which allows the book when open to lie flat.

*****Overlay.**—To make ready by overlaying—the reverse of underlaying.

Overlays.—The term for the special making-ready of an illustration, consisting of several thicknesses of paper cut out according to the nature of the design.

Overplus.—The " plus " or " over " copies of a definite number in printing.

*****Overrun.**—To re-arrange or re-make-up matter after deletions or insertions.

Overs.—The " plus " copies beyond a certain number.

Overseer.—The foreman of any department in a printing office.

"**O.**"—Curtailment of "overseer" of any department in a printing office.

Oversewn.—See " Overcast."

Overtime.—Late or night work that involves an extra charge on labour.

O. T.—An abbreviation for " overtime."

Oxford corners.—Borders with mortised corners, thus **+**

P

Is the fourteenth signature of the printer's alphabet.

PACK.—To paper and string up parcels in the warehouse, or to paper up type or plates.

Pack of cards.—A pack of cards is fifty-two in number.

Packer.—The warehouseman specially told off for packing-up work.

Packing.—A material, generally hemp, used for making tight and sound the joints of steam and other pipes.

P's.—This curtailment stands for " apprentices."

P's and Q's—A novice at case is told to mind his p's and q's owing to the similarity in shape between the letters.

*Page.—A portion of type of a given size made up into shape for printing.

P.—An abbreviation for the word " page."

PP.—Plural of abbreviation of p. for " page."

*Page cord.—A particular kind of cord, about the thickness of twine, used for tying up pages of type.

Page gauge.—A piece of notched reglet used for making-up pages to a uniform length.

*Page hangs.—When a forme is badly locked up the corners of the pages get out of the square and are said to " hang."

*Page paper.—Pieces of stiff paper or wrapper upon which pages of type are placed in order to release galleys.

Paging ink.—A special ink made for paging or numbering machines.

Paging machines.—Mechanical apparatus for automatic numbering.

Pair of cases.—The two cases of type, upper and lower respectively, are said to be a " pair."

*Pale colour.—Sheets printed with an insufficient quantity of ink.

Pallet knife.—An article used for taking ink from the can and for spreading it on the table, or for mixing purposes.

Pamphlet.—Any work which does not exceed five sheets, and is usually done up in a paper wrapper. An extra charge on composition is involved for this class of work.

Pan on.—A slang expression sometimes used by printers to describe anyone with a " fit of the blues."

Pantograph.—An instrument for drawing on reduced or enlarged scales.

Paper (Sizes of).—Regular sizes, such as demy, medium, royal, double foolscap, double crown, imperial, etc.

Paper (Varieties of).—Such as hand-made, machine, drawing, writing, etc.

Paper boards.—A term applied to cheap bindings in boards, but with paper instead of cloth sides.

*Paper boards.—Boards used in the wetting department between the different reams whilst in the screw-press.

*Paper bench.—The bank or " horse " which paper is placed on in the press-room.

Paper cloth.—Paper made with a cloth face to allow of its being folded without breaking.

Paper knife.—A knife used in the warehouse for cutting up paper or for opening the edges of a book.

Paper moulding.—Stereotype moulding by the " paper " or " patent " process.

Paper process.—Stereotyping by means of paper moulds, called the "new" or "patent" process—distinct from "plaster" process.

Paper stereo.—See "Paper process."

*****Paper the case.**—Lining the bottoms of cases—usually done now by the manufacturers before the bottom of the case is fastened on.

*****Paper up.**—To paper up sorts or type for warehousing in store-room.

Papéteries.—French equivalent for stationery.

Papier Ingres.—A French hand-made paper used more especially for drawing purposes.

Papier-maché.—Pulped paper compressed into various shapes.

Papyrograph.—A small mechanical apparatus for duplicating letters, etc., first written by hand upon a prepared substance, and from which a large number of copies can be taken.

Papyrus.—The ancient material for writing purposes, made from a reed which grows in Egypt. Also applied to the old written scrolls.

Paragon.—A size of type one size larger than Great Primer and one size smaller than Double Pica, equalling two Long Primers in depth.

*****Paragraph.**—The commencement of a fresh section by a new line, indicated on MS. by ¶ or [

Paragraph mark.—A reference mark, thus ¶

Pars.—An abbreviation of the word "paragraphs."

Parallel.—A reference mark for foot-notes, indicated thus ‖

Pardoe machine.—A rotary machine adapted for newspaper work invented by Mr. J. Pardoe.

Parenthesis.—A mark of punctuation indicated thus (or)

Par.—Abbreviation used in the reading department for the words "parenthesis" or "paragraph."

Parchment.—Sheepskins prepared for writing or printing purposes.

Particulars of sale.—A class of work which comes under the head of legal or auctioneer's work.

Passing the galley.—In slip work, when a compositor has finished his copy, he passes the galley, if not already filled, to the next in order.

Passing the make-up.—As each compositor finishes his copy he makes up his matter into pages, and then "passes the make-up" to the next in order.

*Paste.—A mucilage made of flour with the addition of a little alum.

Paste and scissors.—Matter copied from journal to journal is sarcastically so termed.

Pasteboard.—Boards made by pasting sheets of paper to any given thickness.

Paste bowl.—The utensil for holding paste.

Paste-downs.—The blank flyleaves, sometimes coloured, at either end of a book which are pasted down on the covers.

Paste points.—Very fine points—usually drawing pins—used for very closely registered work on a hand-press.

Patch up.—To overlay or bring up an impression sheet with pieces of thin paper.

Patent composition.—See "Patent rollers."

Patent rollers.—Applied to rollers of special composition, protected by letters patent.

Patent type.—The specially hard type made by the Patent Type Founding Co.

*Pearl.—A size of type one size larger than Diamond and one size smaller than Ruby, equalling half a Long Primer in depth —the smallest type enumerated by Moxon.

Pearlash.—Carbonate of potash when diluted is used as a wash for type.

Peculiars.—A general term for out-of-the-way sorts, *i.e.* accents, records, etc.

Pedestal ink table.—A small ink table on a single leg or pedestal.

*****Peel.**—A wooden implement used for hanging up printed sheets for drying.

Peeling.—A process of preparing overlays by skivering or thinning down the hard edges of an illustration.

*****Pelts.**—Sheepskins for covering the old-fashioned balls used in inking type.

Per cent mark.—A commercial sign, thus %

Perfect paper.—Reams of paper made up to a printer's ream, *i.e.* 516 sheets, are said to be " perfect."

Perfect up.—This is the printing of the second side of the paper in half-sheet or sheet work.

Perfecting.—The act of printing the second side of a sheet.

Perfecting machine.—A double cylindrical machine which prints both sides of the sheet at one operation.

Perforating machine.—A mechanical contrivance for perforating purposes.

Perforating rule.—A dotted rule standing high in a forme of type which would partly cut the paper in printing.

Perforation.—To allow of a portion being torn off readily order books and cheque books are generally perforated by small pin-holes.

Period.—This mark of punctuation is technically called a full-point.

Periodicals.—The class of work which embraces journals and magazines, and involves an extra charge in composition.

Permanent colours.—Inks which do not readily fade— used for cheque books, etc.

Persian.—The particular fount of type used for composing works in that language.

Persian cases.—Cases of a special lay for works in that language.

Persian morocco.—An imitation morocco leather.

Photographic cards.—Cards used for mounting photographic prints.

Photography.—A process of chemical printing from glass after development by means of light.

Photo-lithography.—In this process the work is placed on the stone by means of photography instead of being drawn by hand.

Photo-zincography.—Process blocks produced by means of photography on zinc plates.

Phytochromotypy.—A process by means of which plants and leaves are printed on paper.

*Pica.—A size of type one size larger than Small Pica and one size smaller than English—the body usually taken as a standard for leads, width of measures, etc.—it is equal to two Nonpareils in body.

Pica clumps.—Pieces of metal of that depth in body.

Pica reglet.—Wooden furniture of that depth in body.

Pick brush.—A small stiff brush used for cleansing type.

Pick sorts.—To take any particular scarce letter from good or bad matter in order to obviate distribution.

Picker.—A corrector or finisher of stereotype plates. In olden times a fine bodkin was thus termed.

Picking.—Touching up or repairing stereo or electro plates.

*Picks.—A speck or blur caused by dirt or badly distributed ink on the face of a letter.

*Pie.—Type broken or indiscriminately mixed.

Piece-work.—Work paid for by result, in accordance with a fixed scale of charges, distinct from time-work or 'stab.

Piece.—Abbreviation for "piece-work."

Piecing leads.—In wide measures of type the leads required are usually pieced, because long leads are apt to get bent or broken.

Pigeon holes.—Receptacles for type and sorts in the store-room.

*Pigeon holes.—A slang expression used by compositors for wide and bad spacing, on account of the amount of white between the words.

Piggery.—A slang expression used by compositors to define a press-room.

*Pigh.—Another way of spelling the word " pie," occasionally used.

Pigs.—Pressmen are thus denominated by compositors in order to annoy them.

Pigsty.—A press-room is sometimes thus designated by compositors.

*Pile of books.—A stack of books bound or in sheets—if gathered.

*Pile of paper (or **work**).—A stack of printed or unprinted paper.

Pinched post.—A size of writing paper, small post, 19 × 14½ inches.

Pinion.—A small wheel, such as a cog, working within a larger one.

Pin mark.—This is the slight mark in the side of a type near the top of the shank made in casting by machinery.

Pins.—The French brads or nails used for mounting plates on wood.

Pirie's paper.—Mostly applied to the writing papers of various kinds made by Messrs. Pirie and Sons of Aberdeen.

Piston.—A small cylinder which works in and out, fixed in the larger cylinder of the engine, and which conveys the motion to machinery by means of a rod.

Piston rod.—The connection between the piston and machinery which imparts motion.

Pit.—The hollow cavity in the floor under a machine for accessibility to the under parts. It is sometimes also necessary for the steady working of a machine.

Pitch.—Placing the forme on a machine to a given position, in order that the type will be printed correctly on the sheet.

Placards.—The class of small poster work, such as showbills, etc.

Planer.—A flat smooth piece of wood used for levelling the type before locking-up.

Planing down.—The act of levelling the type by means of the wooden planer.

Planing machine.—A machine used for planing the backs of stereo plates or squaring up plates and blocks.

Plant.—This term covers the whole of the working material of a printer—machines, type, etc.

Plaster stereo.—Stereotype plates cast from plaster moulds.

Plate marked.—The impression mark of the outer edge beyond the printed part of a copper-plate.

Plate paper.—Soft paper of good quality used for woodcut printing.

***Platen.**—That part of the press or machine which comes down on the forme and gives the impression.

Platen machine.—Printing machines which have a flat impression—not a cylindrical one.

Plates.—A general term for stereo or electro plates.

Plates.—Illustrations of any kind inserted in books.

Platten.—Another mode of spelling the word "Platen," which see.

Plough.—An instrument used for cutting the edges of a book.

Plug.—To repair any damage to a woodcut it is necessary to "plug" the block and re-engrave.

Plus.—The over copies to any given number in printing off.

Plus mark.—A sign in arithmetic, thus ✛

*Point holes.—The punctures made in the sheets by the pins or spurs of the points.

*Point screws.—Screws for fastening the points on the tympan.

Pointer.—The layer-on on a machine who "points" the second side of a sheet in printing.

*Points.—An expression applied generally to all marks of punctuation.

*Points.—Long thin pieces of iron with a pin or spur at the end, used for ensuring the correct register of the sheets in perfecting.

Pole.—A slang expression for a wages bill.

Poles.—A series of wooden poles for drying printed work.

Polling backwards.—When a compositor designedly retards the finishing of his copy in order to secure a better take next time, even though he may lose more in the end by idling.

Polton's paper.—A particular kind of machine writing paper wire-marked with that name.

'Pos.—An abbreviation for the word apostrophe—a mark of punctuation.

Post.—A size of printing paper, 20 × 16 inches; see Large post and Small post respectively.

Postal tubes.—Tubes of various sizes, made of paper or thin strawboard, for protecting paper or prints going through the post.

Postcard size.—The official size for inland cards is $4\frac{1}{4}$ × 3 inches; for foreign, $5\frac{1}{2}$ × $3\frac{1}{2}$ inches.

Posters.—The class of work used for posting up on hoardings —large broadsides, etc.

Poster chases.—Large chases without cross-bars adapted for broadside work.

Poster stick.—A long wooden composing stick.

Pott.—A size of writing paper, 15½ × 12½ inches; printing paper, 16 × 13 inches.

Pouncey's paper.—A particular kind of writing paper manufactured by the maker of that name.

Pound mark.—The sign for pound sterling—£; for weight, ℔.

Preliminary.—Any matter coming before the main text of a work—title, preface, contents, etc.

*Press.—A hand machine for printing or for pressing.

*Press blankets.—Blankets used as tympans. They are sometimes laid in between the two tympans when made of other material.

*Press boards.—Generally the boards used in the wetting press.

*Press girthing.—The webbing which checks the running in or out of the press carriage.

*Press goes.—When the pressmen are at work and in "full swing."

Press lock-up chases.—Large chases specially made to allow of small jobs being locked-up inside them on the press.

Press pin.—The bar used for tightening up the screw-press.

Press plates.—The iron plates placed at intervals in the hydraulic press.

Press proof.—The final proof passed by the author or publisher "for press."

Press revise.—The final proof for press or machine.

Press reviser.—The reader who revises the final proofs.

Press rollers.—The rollers used at press, as distinguished from machine rollers.

Press room (or department).—The part of a printing office occupied by the hand-presses.

*Press work.—A general term for work executed by hand-press.

Presses (Varieties of).—Albion, Columbian, Stanhope, Alexandra, etc.

Pressing boards.—The glazed boards used for pressing printed sheets.

*****Pressmen.**—The skilled workmen who manipulate hand-presses.

Prestonian machine.—A rotary machine adapted for newspaper work, and equally available for type or stereotype plates.

Prima.—In reading a work sheet by sheet the first word of the ensuing signature is marked by the reader as the "prima."

Prince of Wales note paper.—A size of writing paper, $4\frac{1}{2} \times 3$ inches.

Print.—Compositors sometimes speak of work as " print."

*****Printers' devil.**—A term generally applied to the junior apprentice in a printing office.

Printers' marks.—In olden times many printers had their own particular signs, and were identified by these marks.

Printers' ream.—A perfect ream of 516 sheets.

Printery.—An Americanism for a printing office.

*****Printing.**—The art of imprinting type on paper by means of ink.

*****Printing house.**—A more ancient term for a printing office.

*****Printing inks.**—Pigments of various colours for taking a readable impression from type.

Printing offices.—The more modern expression for printing houses.

Printing papers.—Papers of a cheaper description specially used for printing purposes, distinct from hand-made or drawing papers.

Prints.—Illustrations or plates in a book.

Process blocks.—Illustrations in relief produced by any mechanical process.

Process work.—Applied to blocks made by mechanical means.

Prog.—An abbreviation of the word "prognosticate" very frequently used by printers.

*Proof.—A trial print of any forme of type, plates, or blocks.

Proof paper.—A commoner description of printing paper used for taking trial proofs.

*Proof press.—A hand-press used exclusively for pulling proofs.

Proof puller.—The person told off for this particular duty.

Proof reader.—A general term for the "corrector of the press."

*Proof sheet.—Applied to the preliminary prints for reading purposes.

Proofs in sheets.—Proofs of matter made up into pages imposed and pulled in sheet form, as distinct from slip proofs.

Proofs in slips.—Where corrections and alterations are likely to be heavy, proofs are asked for in "slip" form—not made up into pages.

Prov.—An abbreviation for the word "provident," a fund established for unemployed workmen by their trade society.

Provincial houses.—A general term for expressing printing offices out of London.

Publications.—Periodicals and such like. This class of work has a special charge in "casting up."

Publishers' binding.—An ordinary term used for cloth binding.

Puff.—A recognized term for an advertisement in ordinary matter—anything obliquely praised.

*Pulled home.—When the bar of a hand-press is pulled right over so as to touch the near side cheek.

Puller.—That one of the pair who work at a printing press who pulls the press over.

Pulley.—A small wheel on which any part of a machine or tape revolves.

Pull out.—A somewhat slangy expression used as a direction to make more haste.

Pull over.—The act of bringing the bar-handle of a press over.

*****Pulls.**—A term applied generally to proofs or copies of a forme.

Pulp boards.—Cardboards made from pulp of any thickness —not pasteboard.

*****Punches.**—The small steel dies used for punching into the matrix.

*****Punctuation.**—The art of giving sense to composition by marks of punctuation. It is generally termed pointing by printers.

*****Punctuation (Marks of).**—All points used in punctuation come under this head.

Put down.—To alter any words with capitals to lower case.

Put in.—To distribute type ready for composition.

Put up.—To alter lower case to capitals. See " Put down."

Put up overlays.—To place the making ready of cuts on a machine.

*****Pye.**—Another way of spelling the word " pie."

Q

Is the fifteenth signature of the printer's alphabet.

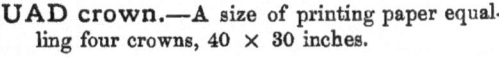**UAD crown.**—A size of printing paper equalling four crowns, 40 × 30 inches.

Quad demy.—A size of printing paper equalling four demys, 45 × 35 inches.

Quad foolscap.—A size of printing paper equalling four foolscaps, 34 × 27 inches.

Quad large.—Cards equalling four "large," 9 × 6 inches.

Quad medium.—A size of printing paper equalling four mediums, 48 × 38 inches.

Quad out.—To run out or fill up a line with quadrats.

Quad post.—A size of printing paper equalling four posts, 40 × 32 inches.

Quad pott.—A size of printing paper equalling four potts, 32 × 26 inches.

Quad royal.—A size of printing paper equalling four royals, 50 × 40 inches.

Quad small.—Cards equalling four "smalls," 7 × 5 inches.

Quadrant.—A small crescent-shaped piece of iron or steel used for the movement of the vibrating roller on a platen machine.

Quadrant machines.—A small cylindrical printing machine adapted for jobbing purposes made by Messrs. Powell and Son.

*Quadrats.—Large metal spaces of various sizes for filling up short lines, etc.

Quadrats (Sizes of).—One, two, three, and four ems of any particular body.

Quad.—A very general abbreviation of the word "quadrat." Also used as a short term for "quadruple."

*Quadrat-high.—Anything, such as spaces or furniture, made to the height of quadrats.

Quadruple.—Any sheet made four times the size of a smaller sheet, such as quad-demy, etc.

*Quarter.—This has reference to a particular corner of a forme or chase—the cross-bars generally dividing the chase into four equal sections.

Quarter bound.—Books bound with back only in leather.

*Quarto.—A size given when a sheet is folded into four leaves —written shortly, 4to.

Quarto galley.—A wide galley suitable for works of that size—distinct from slip galley.

Quaternions.—Paper folded in sections of four sheets, quire fashion.

Queen note paper.—A size of writing paper, $5\frac{3}{8} \times 3\frac{1}{4}$ inches.

*Qui.—Notice to quit—contraction of "quietus."

Quinternions.—Paper folded in sections of five sheets, quire fashion.

*Quire.—Sections of a ream of paper, consisting of twenty-four sheets.

Quire fashion.—See "Quirewise."

Quire folded.—See "Quired paper."

Quires.—Books in sheets, *i.e.* not bound, are said to be in quires.

Quired paper.—Reams of paper folded in quires—not sent in "flat."

Quirewise.—Jobs of single leaves printed on both sides of the paper, *i.e.* as first and third pages. This allows of "sewing" instead of "stabbing."

Quoin drawer.—The receptacle for holding quoins in the imposing stone.

Quoin drawer overseer.—A name given to the compositor who makes up furnitures, etc.

Quoin up.—To fit quoins preparatory to locking-up the forme.

*Quoins.—Small wedges of various sizes, usually of wood, used for tightening or locking-up formes.

*Quotation justifiers.—Spaces for justifying lines of quotations.

*Quotation quadrats.—Another name for quotations.

*Quotations.—Large quadrats, generally of four-line pica and cast hollow, used for making up blanks and short pages.

*Quoted matter.—Extracts and other matter placed between "inverted commas."

*Quotes.—The turned commas (") and apostrophes (") used respectively for quoted matter.

R

Is the sixteenth signature of the printer's alphabet.

**ACK.**—A row of teeth placed horizontally which cog-wheels fit into as the coffin of a machine runs in and out.

*Racks.—Receptacles for holding cases, boards, etc.

*Rag.—The bur sometimes left on type by the founder used to be thus called.

Rags.—Pieces of old linen or calico used for cleaning machinery.

Railway buff paper.—A common machine-made paper of buff colour, very strong in texture—generally used by railway and other carriers for delivery sheets, etc.

Ralph.—Another name for the "spirit" or evil genius of the "chapel."

Random.—A special frame used by compositors in making-up and for putting standing lines and heads on.

Range matter.—To make lines in composing range equally at either or both ends of the stick.

Ranks.—Composing frames are generally arranged in rows or ranks, and a compositor is facetiously said to belong to the "ranks."

Rat.—A slang term for a compositor who works at a lower rate of wages than that generally recognized in a particular locality.

Ratchet wheel.—A small cog-wheel used in the smaller working parts of a machine.

Ratting.—Working at less than recognized scale prices.

*****Reader.**—The responsible person who compares and reads the proof by copy, and who also revises corrections made by an author or editor. Also called "corrector of the press."

*****Reader's marks.**—The corrections and alterations—errors and deviations from copy or style—marked on a proof, and distinct from "author's marks."

Reading boy.—The lad who reads the copy to the reader or "corrector of the press."

*****Reading closet.**—A small compartment within the reading room. Each reader is generally allotted a separate place in order to secure a certain amount of quietness.

Reading for press.—The final stage of reading preparatory to printing.

Reading room.—The department which includes the reading staff.

*****Ream.**—Paper in parcels or bundles of a certain size—a printer's ream being 516 sheets. Hand-made and drawing papers slightly differ in the number of sheets, sometimes 472, 480, or 500.

Reamage.—This term is applied generally to the quantity of a number of reams.

Recipe mark.—A medical sign expressed thus ℞

Reclothing rollers.—Substituting new composition for old on the stocks.

Records.—Applied to the various signs and accents used for old works, thus, ă ē ĭ p m̂ etc.

Recto.—The right-hand pages of any work.

Red edges.—The edges of books are sometimes coloured red and burnished.

Reel of paper.—The paper made in continuous lengths used for rotary printing machines.

Reference marks.—Those signs which are used for foot-notes, as * † ‖ etc. Sometimes superior letters or figures are substituted.

*Register.—The exact adjustment of pages back to back in printing the second side of a sheet.

*Register sheets.—The impressions from a forme used in obtaining correct register.

*Reglet.—Thin wooden furniture up to Two-line Great Primer generally comes under the head of " reglet."

Reglet (Sizes of).—Most sizes of types have their equivalent in reglets.

*Reiteration.—The second side of a sheet in printing.

Reit (or Ret).—A short term for the word " reiteration," the reverse side of a sheet in printed work.

Relative weights.—The difference in weight of any reams between printing, writing, or drawing papers.

Relief printing.—Letterpress and block printing comes under the head of " relief," as distinct from lithography or plate printing.

Religious marks.—Signs such as ✠ ℞ ♉

Removes.—The difference between one size of type and another is expressed by this term.

Renewing rollers.—When rollers are worn out, the stocks are " reclothed," or " renewed " with composition.

Reprint copy.—Printed copy is called " reprint," as distinct from MS., and a lower price is paid for it in composition.

R. P.—These initials stand for " reprint."

Reprints.—Applied generally to works printed for the second or any subsequent edition.

Response.—A sign used in prayer books and other religious works, and expressed thus ℞

Retree.—The outside, rejected, or damaged paper of different reams, marked thus × × in invoicing.

*Revise.—A second or subsequent proof.

Reviser.—The reader who revises proofs.

*Ribs.—The framework on which the press carriage runs in and out.

*Ride.—When leads are pieced in wide measures they sometimes shift and overlap each other. They are then said to "ride."

Rider.—A rod attached to the "inker" roller on a printing machine.

Rider.—An insertion in copy of additional MS. marked to come in at a certain place.

Riggers.—Wheels attached to shafting for transmitting driving power to a machine.

Right-hand pages.—Those pages with odd folios, *e.g.* 1, 3, 5, 7, etc. Also called "recto."

*Riglet.—Another and older form of spelling the word "reglet."

*Rinsing trough.—The trough in which formes are washed.

*Rise.—A forme is said to rise when it springs through bad locking up and the type gets off its feet. The term is also used when quadrats and furniture black in printing through imperfect justification.

Risers.—Wooden or metal blocks for mounting stereo and other plates.

Rod.—A long straight piece of iron or steel connecting two working parts of machinery.

Roll.—To calender or glaze paper or printed work.

Rolled paper.—The class of paper glazed or calendered for cut work, etc.

Roller box.—The receptacle in which rollers are kept to protect them from dust, etc.

Roller composition.—A compound mainly made of treacle and glue.

1

Roller cupboard.—A cupboard in which rollers are stored to protect them from glare and dust.

Roller forks.—The contrivance which holds the roller when working in a printing machine.

Roller frame.—The iron frame which press rollers are fitted into.

Roller ink.—A common black ink used for the preservation of press rollers when out of use.

Roller knife.—An implement used for scraping off the preservative "roller" ink when the roller is required for use.

Roller moulds.—Apparatus of various sizes in which rollers are cast.

Roller racks.—Receptacles for storing rollers when not in use.

Roller sockets.—The open part of the roller fork in which the spindle rests.

Roller spindle.—The iron rod on which rollers revolve on the frame or forks.

Roller stocks.—Generally made of wood and on which the composition is cast.

Roller stop.—A contrivance on a printing machine for stopping or fixing rollers whilst in motion.

Roller throw-off.—An appliance for stopping or throwing off rollers whilst a machine is running.

Roller washing.—The act of cleansing rollers.

Roller wheel.—The wheels on which the rollers revolve in a printing machine.

Rollers.—The apparatus for distributing and applying the ink to a forme in printing.

Rolling machine.—A machine for glazing or calendering paper or printed work.

Rolling washing trough.—A special trough made for this purpose.

*Roman.—The particular kind of type in which book and other work is composed (such as this fount), as distinguished from *italic* or fancy types. Called "antiqua" by the Germans,

*Roman cases.—The cases for these founts as distinguished from *italic* cases.

Roman numerals.—The pagination of the preliminary matter of a volume is generally expressed by these characters, thus—i, ii, iii, iv, etc.

Ronde.—A fancy character of type somewhat similar to a script.

Rope paper.—Strong packing paper of various sizes made largely of old rope.

Rotary gatherer.—A revolving circular table for gathering sheets into books.

Rotary machine.—Cylindrical machines for printing from a continuous roll or web of paper.

Rotary.—A short term for rotary printing machines.

Rotten.—Term applied to unsound impression in printing.

*Rounce.—The handle by means of which the press carriage is run in and out.

Royal.—A size of printing paper, 25 × 20 inches; writing paper, 24 × 19 inches.

*Rub out ink.—To rub by means of the brayer the ink on the ink table previous to distribution.

Rubber stamps.—Hand stamps cast in vulcanized india-rubber.

Rubber type.—Separate types cast in vulcanized india-rubber and generally mounted on metal bodies.

Rubrics.—The directions placed in a prayer book, which were formerly—and are now sometimes—printed in red ink.

Rubricated letters.—Capital letters printed in red ink.

Rubricated matter.—Sentences or paragraphs printed in red ink.

Ruby.—A size of type one size larger than Pearl and one size smaller than Nonpareil, equal to half a Small Pica in body.

Ruck.—A sheet is said to "ruck" when it gets creased or doubled in laying on.

Rule borders.—A frame, usually of brass rule, fitted round a page.

Rule case.—Trays for holding brass rule of the usual size of type cases.

Rule cutter.—An apparatus for cutting brass rule into short lengths.

Rule work.—Composition in which rules are largely used, such as table-work, which see.

Ruled paper.—Papers of different kinds with various rulings, used for account books, etc.

*Rules.—A general term for rules—brass, type, or wood.

Ruling.—The art of printing lines in any colour or direction on paper.

Ruling machine.—The apparatus for ruling purposes.

Run a waste through.—This is done in order to get good and even "colour" before starting printing.

*Run in carriage.—To move the forme carriage or coffin under the platen or cylinder.

*Run on.—An intimation that a sentence is not to commence a fresh paragraph, or chapters are not to commence on a different page.

Run on chapters.—An intimation that the commencement of chapters in a work are not necessarily to begin on a fresh page.

Run on solid.—To continue without break or leads any particular matter.

*Run on sorts.—An extraordinary demand for any particular letter or letters in composing.

*Run out.—To fill up or "run out" a line with quadrats or full points.   Also to "run out" of sorts.

Run out and indent.—To set matter the reverse of ordinary paragraphs by putting the first line full out and indenting the subsequent lines.

*Run out carriage.—To move back the forme carriage or coffin from under the platen or cylinder.

Run out with full points.—To fill up a line with full points, as in "contents" matter.

Run out with leaders.—To fill up a line with "leaders."

Run out with quads.—To fill up a line with quadrats.

Run up colour.—To distribute ink and to prepare for printing.

*Runs in.—Matter is said to "run in" when it "gets in," or makes less than an anticipated quantity.

Runners.—In press-work a line of corks to prevent the roller from depositing an excess of ink on the edges of the pages. In a machine, a flat row of teeth for working cog-wheels in.

Runners.—Figures or letters placed down the length of a page to indicate the particular number or position of any given line.

Running headline.—The fixed or general title of the volume as distinct from the chapter or section headline.

Running title.—See "Running headline."

Runic.—A character of type between Greek and Gothic.

Russia.—A leather largely used for binding books.

Russian.—The particular character of type used for composing works in that language.

Russian cases.—Cases of special lay for type used in composing that language.

Ruthven press.—This was a hand-press patented by Mr. Ruthven many years ago. Its principle consisted in the platen being brought over the forme, which was stationary, instead of the forme being run in.

S

Is the seventeenth signature of the printer's alphabet.

SAFETY-VALVE.—This is a valve through which steam would escape if its pressure exceeded the maximum power, and thus give warning of danger.

Samaritan.—An ancient character of letter said to have been used by the early Hebrews, types of which can be obtained.

Samaritan cases.—Cases of special lay used for composing works in that language.

Samples.—This term is generally applied to pattern or specimen sheets of paper.

Sanscrit.—The ancient language of Hindostan. Types of its written characters can be obtained.

Sanscrit cases.—Cases of special lay for composing works in that language.

Sat.—Abbreviation of the word "satisfaction," sometimes used by printers to express a revengeful feeling.

Saw.—The small tenon saw used for cutting up furniture, etc. It also sometimes refers to the "circular saw."

Saw bench.—The stand or table where the sawing is done.

Saw block.—A block of wood in which slots are cut, used for sawing up furniture on.

*Saxon.—The particular character of type used for composing works in that language.

Saxon cases.—Cases of special lay used for composing works in that language.

*Scabbard.—An old term for the more modern word "scale-board," which see.

Scabby.—A term applied to uneven and rotten colour in printing.

*Scale-board.—Very thin strips of wooden furniture used for obtaining close register in printing.

Scale price.—Specific prices adjusted to the recognized scale as agreed to by employers and employed, varying according to locality.

Scandinavian.—A printing machine with single cylinder, introduced many years ago into this country by the inventor—a Scandinavian.

Scan.—A short term for the "Scandinavian" printing machine.

Scarce sorts.—Any particular letter or letters which are in great demand through a "run on sorts."

Scissors.—The ordinary domestic implements—used by printers in making ready at press or machine.

Scoring machine.—A mechanical apparatus for scoring cards to allow of folding without breaking.

Scrape up.—To clean a roller by scraping off the coat of protecting ink.

Scratch comma.—A sign thus / used in old documents and reprints. It is now used as a shilling mark.

Scratch figures.—A figure cast with a line through it thus ℈ to indicate a cancel, etc.

Screw chases.—Chases mostly used for newspaper work, fitted with screws to obviate the use of wooden quoins.

Screw composing stick.—The old-fashioned composing stick is fastened up by means of a screw with a slotted head.

Screw hammer.—A tool with a screw attached to the claw, thus allowing it to be used as a spanner or wrench to any width up a certain point.

Screw press.—A press in which the power is obtained by means of a screw.

Screw quoins.—A term for the screw substitutes for wooden quoins.

Screw stick.—See " Screw composing stick."

Script.—Sloping type similar in character to handwriting.

Scroofing.—A slang expression used to denote searching for scarce sorts instead of distributing.

Scruple mark.—A medical sign, thus Э

*Second at press.—At hand-press the partner who subordinates himself to the " first," or leading hand.

*Second forme.—In sheet work the second side in printing.

Seconds mark.—A double acute accent is used for this purpose, thus ″

*Section.—A reference mark for footnotes, thus § It is used also to mark divisions in a chapter.

Sector machine.—A cylindrical printing machine.

Sector.—A short term for the " sector " printing machine.

Selected parchments.—Picked parchments—those used for writing purposes.

Selected vellums.—Picked vellums—those used for writing purposes.

Selenotype.—A fantastic type, sometimes called " chaostype."

Self inking.—Apparatus attached to any machine to dispense with the application of ink by hand.

Semicolon.—A mark of punctuation, thus ;

Sem.—An abbreviation used for the word " semicolon."

Serif.—The fine lines on the top and bottom of a letter, thus H

*Set.—A recognized term for " composed "—to " set " type is to " compose " it.

*Set clean.—Matter composed with few mistakes.

*Set close.—Matter composed with closer than average spacing.

*Set foul.—Matter composed carelessly—the reverse of "clean."

*Set off.—When the ink off-sets from one sheet to another.

Set-off paper.—See " Set-off sheets."

Set-off sheets.—Special sheets used to prevent the off-set from sheet to sheet when printed.

Set out.—To compose all the type out of a case, or to arrange and white out any particular job.

*Set up.—A common term used instead of the word "compose."

Set up close.—When an intervening " take " of copy is finished, it is said to be " set up close," that is, to the next " take."

*Set wide.—To space wider than the average in composing type.

Sets up to himself.—This is a term used when a compositor has received two consecutive " takes " of copy, and thus " sets " up the first to his second portion.

Setting rules.—The brass rules used in setting type and shifted line by line as finished.

Sewer.—The person, usually a female, who does the sewing preparatory to binding.

Sewn.—A term applied to anything sewn—not stitched or stabbed—in binding.

Shafting.—The revolving turned-iron pole suspended horizontally to convey the driving power to the machines.

*Shake.—A slur on a printed sheet through some defect in the impression.

Shammock.—An old expression for to " mike," or to be idle.

*Shank.—The body of the letter or type.

Sharp impression.—Clear and clean impression in printing.

*Shears.—The ordinary implements—used for cutting leads or brass rule.

*Sheepsfoot.—An iron hammer with a claw at the foot.

Sheet and a half.—Regular sizes of paper made to a size half as much again to facilitate and economize in working off odd sizes or odd pages.

Sheet dips.—When a sheet does not lie quite flat, and "dips" into the broken or open spaces of a forme, and either "blacks" or throws the register out.

Sheet the roller.—An operation necessary in order to take off superfluous ink from a roller.

*Sheet work.—Applied to works or jobs printed both sides— the reverse of half-sheet or "work and turn."

Sheeted.—This expression is used when heavily printed work has to be placed sheet by sheet between other sheets to prevent off-set of ink.

Shell.—The thin film of copper that forms the face of an electrotype, and which is afterwards backed up with lead to the required thickness.

Shelving.—To undercharge the amount of work done, and carry it forward to the next week's bill.

Sherwin and Cope's press.—An old iron hand-press, called "Imperial press."

Shilling mark.—The sign thus / which was used in old books as a "scratch comma."

'Ship.—An abbreviation of the word "companionship"—a body of men working on that system.

Shoe.—An old boot or shoe is sometimes used as a receptacle for battered and broken letters.

Shooter.—Short term used for the word "shooting stick."

*Shooting stick.—The implement—generally made of box-wood, but sometimes of metal—used with the mallet in locking-up formes.

Short "and."—The ampersand, thus & (roman), *&* (italic), ₵ ('black letter).

*Short cross.—The shortest and widest of the two cross-bars in any chase.

Short measures.—Narrow widths of type come under this head, such as are used for double or treble columns.

*Short numbers.—Small numbers in printing, such as 250 or 500.

*Short page.—A page of type not the full length of the gauge, as at the end of a chapter, or a line short by reason of the exigencies of making-up.

*Short pull.—When the bar-handle of the press is not pulled over to its full length.

Short sorts.—When there is a run on any particular letter or letters, and they become scarce.

Short takes.—In order to expedite the getting out of work in composing rooms, the men are sometimes given short portions of copy.

Short twelves.—A plan of imposition whereby the pages are laid down in three short rows of four.

Shorts.—A term applied to letters with the " short" accent over them, thus ă ĕ ĭ ŏ ŭ

Shorts.—Applied to copies printed off short of the number required.

Shoulder notes.—Marginal notes placed at the top corner of the page.

*Shoulder of type.—The flat top of the shank of a type from whence the bevel to the face starts.

Shuffling.—Another term for fanning out preparatory to knocking-up work in the warehouse.

Side flues.—The lower flues which run on either side of the boiler and open on to the front.

Side lay.—The margin of a given measurement on one side of a sheet in printing.

Side mark.—The fixed mark at the side which a sheet is laid to in printing on a machine.

Side-notes.—Marginal notes as distinct from " foot-notes."

*Side-sticks.—Sloping sticks of wood used for quoining up against in imposing a forme.

Sigla.—Signs and characters frequently used in ancient MSS., thus 7 ⚹ etc.

*Signature.—The letter or figure in the white line of the first page of a sheet, to guide binder in folding—also used by printers to identify any particular sheet.

Sigs.—A short term for " signatures."

Signature line.—The line of quadrats at the bottom of a page in which the signature letter or figure is placed.

Signature page.—The first page of a sheet, on which the signature appears.

Signs.—Characters used in relation to astronomy, algebra, medicine, etc., come under this head.

Silver bronze.—A metallic powder used for silver printing.

Single cylinder machines.—Machines for printing one side at a time only, as distinct from perfecting or rotary ones.

Single frame.—A half frame for holding only one pair of cases up at a time.

Sit.—An abbreviation for the word " situation," an engagement for work.

Sixteenmo.—A sheet folded into sixteen leaves—written shortly, 16mo.

*Sixteens.—A familiar way of expressing " sixteenmo."

Sixteen-to-pica leads.—Very thin leads cast sixteen to a pica, and called " hair leads."

Six-to-pica brass.—Brass rule cast six to a Pica.

Six-to-pica leads.—Leads cast six to a Pica.

Sixty-fourmo.—A sheet folded into sixty-four leaves—written shortly, 64mo.

Size.—The preparation used for printing with bronze.

Sized paper.—Paper made with a certain proportion of size added, according to instructions for a "hard" or "soft" sized article.

Sizes of cards.—Such as thirds, town, small, large, etc.

Sizes of jobs.—Different sizes, as octavo, quarto, folio, etc.

Sizes of paper.—Regular sizes, as pott, foolscap, demy, medium, royal, imperial, etc., also made in double and quadruple.

Sizes of type.—See Minnikin, Brilliant, Gem, Diamond, Pearl, Ruby, Nonpareil, Minion, Brevier, Bourgeois, Long Primer, Small Pica, Pica, English, Great Primer, Paragon, Double Pica, Two-line Pica, etc.

Skeleton face.—Thin-faced letter used for jobbing purposes.

Skeleton forme.—A special forme—usually of a broken and open nature—made up for a subsequent printing in another colour of ink.

Skinks.—An old term applied to drink—or drinking around the imposing stone in order to celebrate some auspicious occasion.

Slab.—The surface on which the ink is distributed.

*Slice.—A flat wide iron knife used for lifting ink out of the can.

Slice galley.—An old-fashioned galley with a thin additional bottom to facilitate the sliding of pages on to the imposing stone.

Slip chases.—Long narrow chases made specially for "heading" work.

Slip galley.—A long galley the reverse of a quarto or square galley.

Slips.—Applied to matter not made up into pages, but pulled as proofs in long slips.

Slog on.—When a person is working hurriedly he is said to have a "slog on "—a slang expression,

Slugs.—Numbered divisions of metal between different takes of copy.

Slumming.—A slang term used to describe the secreting of type or sorts.

*****Slur.**—When a printed sheet is blurred or smeared—also called a "shake."

*****Small capitals.**—The smaller capitals laid in the upper case, distinct from the full capitals, thus—PRINTING, and indicated in MS. by two lines = underneath.

Small caps.—Short term for "Small capitals," which see.

Small cap. O.—An expression frequently used for an under- or sub-overseer.

Small cards.—A size of card, $3\frac{1}{2}$ × $2\frac{1}{2}$ inches.

Small court envelopes.—Envelopes to take small post 8vo in half, $4\frac{3}{4}$ × $3\frac{1}{4}$ inches.

Small double post.—A size of printing paper, 29 × 19 inches.

Small-faced figures.—Figures of any particular size cast on a larger body than the fount they belong to.

Small hand paper.—A common machine-made paper, generally straw-coloured, used for post wrappers and such purposes.

*****Small numbers.**—Short numbers, as 250 and 500, in printing, as distinguished from "long numbers."

*****Small Pica.**—A size of type one size larger than Long Primer and one size smaller than Pica, equal to half the body of a Double Pica.

Small post.—A size of writing paper, $16\frac{1}{2}$ × $13\frac{1}{2}$ inches.

*****Smout.**—A compositor who seeks odd jobs in various houses. See "Grass hand."

*Soaking pull.—A long and easy pull over of the bar-handle of a printing press.

Society hands.—Those belonging to and working under the rules of a trade society.

Soc.—An abbreviation for the word "society,"—the trade society.

Society houses.—Establishments conforming to the rules and paying the recognized scale price for work.

Soft brass.—Brass rule which can be easily manipulated, specially manufactured for fancy work.

Soft paper.—Paper distinct from hard or sized paper.

*Soft pull.—An easy pull over of the bar-handle of a printing press.

Soft sized paper.—Special printing paper manufactured with a very little admixture of size.

Soft tints.—The lighter parts of an illustration.

*Solace.—A penalty imposed by the chapel for the infringement of any of its rules.

Solid dig.—A lean or bad "take" of copy.

Solid matter.—Type composed without leads; also applied to type with but few quadrats in.

Solids.—The blacker or more solid parts of a woodcut or other illustration.

S. O. papers.—An abbreviation for the special class of papers used by the government "stationery office."

*Sop the balls.—An expression used when too much ink was taken on the balls.

*Sorts.—The general term applied to any particular letter or letters as distinguished from a complete fount.

Soundings.—Pressmen are said to be in "soundings" when they get near the bottom of their heap and their knuckles rap the horse.

Soupy.—A term of disparagement applied to thin or poor ink.

S. p.—An abbreviation used for " small paper" when there are two or more sizes of paper used for any work.

Space barge.—A piece of card or thick paper used to hold spaces on whilst correcting a forme.

Space box.—A small tray with six or eight divisions—a handy substitute for the " space barge."

Space lines.—Leads used for spacing out are sometimes thus termed.

*Space out.—To widen or open out space between words or lines.

Space paper.—Another term for " space barge."

Space rules.—Plain or fancy rules cast type high for filling up blank spaces and dividing sections or chapters.

*Spaces.—Metal blanks cast to different thicknesses of their own bodies for placing between words and filling up lines.

Spaces (Sizes of).—Thick, middling, thin, and hair spaces.

Spanish n.—A capital or lower case n with a curly accent, thus—ñ.

Spanners.—The tool used for fastening or unfastening any nut or screw attached to a machine.

Spatterwork.—A method of transferring leaves of plants or any metal letters to paper.

Specimen page.—In order to decide the shape, size, and style of a new work it is usual to submit a sample page.

Speed riggers.—Riggers graduated to allow of the driving band being shifted to increase or reduce the running power.

*Spirit.—The evil genius of a chapel. See " Ralph."

Split fractions.—Fractional figures cast on two separate bodies to allow of the figure being readily changed, thus—$\frac{1}{2}$ $\frac{1}{2}$ $\frac{1}{12}$.

Split rigger.—Riggers made in two equal portions and screwed together in order to facilitate shifting or changing.

K

Spoilage.—Applied to the sheets spoilt in printing, sometimes called " waste."

*Sponge.—The ordinary domestic article used in damping type for distribution.   Also for sponging rollers.

Sponge up.—Rollers when stale are sometimes improved by sponging with cold water.

Spottiswoode press.—An old platen printing machine invented by Mr. Andrew Spottiswoode.

Spring.—The mechanism which gives a recoil to any press or machine.

Spring box.—The receptacle at the head of the press holding the spring which acts on the bar-handle.

Spring brass.—Rules cast in flexible brass—the reverse of " soft " or " bending " brass rule.

Spring of a forme.—A forme of type or plates is liable to " spring," or go off its feet, if not properly locked up.

Spring points.—These are a special kind of press points which assist in throwing the sheet off the spur of the point as printed.

Sprinkled edges.—Cut edges of books are sometimes finely sprinkled with colour to prevent them getting soiled.

Spur.—The short pin at the end of the point which pricks the hole in the sheet for registering purposes.

*Squabble.—To break or upset type and thus make " pie " of it.

Square twelves.—Twelvemo laid down in imposition the " short " or " square " way, in contradistinction to " long twelves."

Squashed.—Another term for " squabbled " type.

'Stab.—A term applied to establishment hands, *i.e.* workmen paid by the week and not by piece-work.

Stabbed.—A form of stitching by piercing or stabbing, used mostly for cheap pamphlet work.

Stacks.—Paper or printed work arranged in "stacks." See "Pile."

Stage.—A wooden platform a few inches high used for building stacks of paper or printed work on.

Staining paper.—An euphemism for "printing," used as a toast at festivals of master printers in the olden time.

Stamps.—A somewhat amateurish synonym for type.

Standard machine.—A small jobbing cylindrical machine made by Mr. F. Ullmer.

Standing.—Formes not distributed after printing are said to be "standing."

*Standing press.—Screw presses used in the warehouse for pressing.

Stands high.—In printing, type or blocks not to correct height, but a little too high.

Stands low.—The reverse of "stands high," which see.

*Stands still.—A press or machine out of use. Also a workman delayed or out of work.

Stanhope press.—The first iron platen hand-press, invented by Earl Stanhope in the early part of this century.

Staple of press.—The frame or uprights of a hand printing press.

Star.—An asterisk, thus * (used as a reference or otherwise).

Start.—Leaves of books are said to "start" when the sewing is defective and the leaves are loose.

Start working.—To commence working or printing a fresh sheet or job on press or machine.

Steam chest.—The small inverted chest placed on the top of the boiler in which the steam accumulates before passing from the boiler.

Steam cocks.—The taps in front of the boiler by which the steam can be tested.

Steam engine.—The motor driven by means of this power.

Steam gauge.—The dial which indicates the pressure of steam in the boiler.

Steam gearing.—The apparatus in connection with a machine for driving it by steam power, *i.e.* the rigger, striker, etc.

Steam jacketing.—A composition coating laid on the boiler to keep the heat in.

Steam pipes.—Special wrought-iron pipes adapted for steam, generally painted red.

Steam printing.—Any kind of printing executed by means of that power—the reverse of hand-work.

Steel composing rules.—See " Steel rules."

Steel quoins.—A patented mechanical contrivance for locking up formes by means of a key applied to shaped pieces of steel which fit in a kind of rack.

Steel rules.—Composing rules are sometimes made of this material.

***Stem of letter.**—The up and down strokes of any letter.

Stereotypes.—Casts of pages of type, etc., in metal, either by the " plaster " or " paper " processes.

Stereo.—A short term for the word " stereotypes."

Stereo apparatus.—Plant and tools necessary for stereotyping.

Stereo catches.—Short pieces, generally of brass, with a shoulder for holding plates in the required position.

Stereo chases.—Special chases made for use in stereotyping.

Stereo clumps.—Type-high pieces of metal which protect the edges of pages and form the bevel of the plate.

Stereo flong.—The prepared paper which forms the matrix or mould for stereotyping by the paper process.

Stereo furniture.—Metal furniture used for stereotyping purposes.

Stereo metal.—The metal used for stereotyping, as distinct from type-metal, which is of better and harder quality.

Stereo metal blocks.—Metal "risers" or blocks on which to impose stereotype plates.   See "French furniture."

Stereo mounting boards.—A large board—usually of mahogany—on which sets of plates are fastened down to a certain gauge.

Stereo mounts.—The material—wood or metal—used for mounting stereotype plates.

Stereo pins.—The brads or "French tacks" used for fastening stereotype or electrotype plates on blocks.

Stereo wood blocks.—Wooden blocks with brass catches on which stereotype plates are mounted—distinct from "metal" blocks.

Stet.—A Latin word used to denote the cancelling of any correction marked in copy or proof, and indicated by dots underneath, thus . . . . . .

*Stick.—A familiar expression for "composing stick."

*Stickful.—When the composing stick is full, the quantity of type is thus termed.

Sticks.—A slang term used by printers for rollers when out of condition.

Stitched.—A form of fastening up pamphlets, as distinct from "sewing" or "stabbing."

Stock room.—The department allotted to the storing of paper or printed stock.

Stokehole.—The place—often not better than a hole—where the stoker attends to the fire.

*Stone.—A short term used for either stone or iron imposing surfaces.

*Stool.—A platform or stage on which paper or printed work is stacked.

Stop impression.—The arrangement applied to a machine for throwing off the impression whilst it is running.

Stopping cylinder.—A mechanical contrivance for stopping or fixing the cylinder whilst the machine is running.

*Stops (points).—A general term embracing all punctuation marks.

Store-keeper.—The person responsible for the care of type and other materials in a printing office.

Store-room.—The department for storing type, leads, furniture, etc.

Straight accents.—Another term for long accents, thus— ā ē ī ō ū

Straight-edge.—A long wooden or metal stick used for squaring up the pages in a forme in order to obtain correct register in printing.

Strawboard.—Yellow boards of various weights used for binding purposes, principally made of straw.

Striker.—The apparatus attached to a machine for "striking on," or putting it in motion.

Strikes.—A term for type matrices struck from the original punches.

String.—A slang word much used by printers to express a hoax or "sell."

*Strip a forme.—To take away the furniture from the pages of a forme, and thus leave it naked.

Stroker.—A small implement, generally made of wood and tipped with metal, for "stroking in," or laying on sheets in a printing machine.

Stroker in.—The layer-on who strokes in the sheets one by one to be printed.

Strokes.—The up and down lines of any letter.

*Strong ink.—See "Hard ink."

Style of the house.—Most printing offices have their own particular method in the matter of display, spelling, etc.

Sub-title.—The bastard or half-title placed before the general title of a work. Also called "fly-title."

*Summer.—A piece of wood fastened under the ribs of a wooden press close to the "winter."

Sun machine.—A small platen jobbing machine—for treadle or steam—made by Messrs. Greenwood and Batley.

Sunday work.—An extra charge beyond overtime money is charged for working on this day.

Super-calendered paper.—Highly rolled paper for dry printing.

Superior figures.—Small figures cast on the shoulder of type, generally used for footnote reference, thus—[1] [2] [3]

*Superior letters.—Small letters cast at the top of the shoulder of type, used for references or abbreviations, as M[r], N[o], etc. See "Cock-up."

Superiors.—A short term embracing both superior letters and superior figures.

Super royal.—A size of printing paper, $27\frac{1}{2} \times 20\frac{1}{2}$ inches; writing, 27×19 inches.

Surface.—A short term for imposing surface or "stone."

Surface boards.—See "Surface cards."

Surface cards.—Cardboards not coloured right through, but merely the top and bottom sheets, sometimes one side only—distinct from "pulp boards."

Surfaced paper.—Paper with any prepared surface, coloured or otherwise.

*Swash letters.—Seventeenth century italic capitals with tails and flourishes, thus—*A B D M N* etc.

*Sweepings.—Applied to the paper rubbish swept up, and sometimes to the pie picked up from the floor.

Swell rules.—Short fancy rules used as divisions between chapters or sections of a book, thus ━━━

Swifts.—Good and fast compositors were sometimes thus denominated.

Symbols.—Signs or marks peculiar to any particular science.

*Syriac.—The particular founts of type used for composing works in that language.

Syriac case.—Cases of special lay for composing works in that language.

T

Is the eighteenth signature of the printer's alphabet.

ABLE of press.*—The coffin or bed of a press upon which the forme is placed for printing.

Table work.—Matter of four or more columns, which reckons as double composition in casting up.

Tabular work.—Three-column matter, which reckons a quarter or half extra in value of composition according to its nature.

Tacky.—Rollers to be in proper condition ought to be "tacky," that is, should be slightly adhesive to the touch.

Tail-pieces.—Ornaments used for filling up short pages.

Tails.—The bottom or tail-end of a book.

Take.—Each portion of copy falling to the share of a compositor.

Take down.—To take work down from the drying poles in the warehouse department.

Take down.—A somewhat amateurish way of expressing an instruction to distribute or break up type.

*Take up copy.—When a compositor has finished distributing he is said to be ready to "take up copy."

Taker off.—The person, usually a lad, who receives the sheets as printed off, and places them on the heap.

Taking a figure.—A method of balloting by shaking up and drawing certain figures from a workman's apron, in lieu of throwing by quadrats, to determine shares of fat, etc.

*Taking off.—The act of taking the sheets and placing them straight as printed off.

Taking-off apparatus.—The special arrangement for automatically "taking off" the sheets as printed.

Taking-off board.—The board on which the sheets are laid as printed off.

Tape wanders.—When any of the tapes of a machine get astray the fact is thus expressed.

Tapes.—The narrow webbing which carries the sheets from the laying-on to the taking-off board on a machine.

Tea papers.—Ordinary paper cut to set sizes for holding certain weights of that article.

Technical classes.—Classes formed for imparting a practical knowledge of printing.

Technical phrases. — Trade expressions, distinct from "Technical terms," which see.

Technical terms.—Terms applied strictly to trade materials, implements, machinery, etc. See "Technical phrases."

Teeth of cog.—The flange of a cog-wheel, which has its edge cut diamond shape so that it shall fit into the corresponding parts of another wheel.

Ten-to-pica leads.—Leads cast ten to a pica in depth of body.

Ternions.—A bibliographical expression for three sheets folded together in folio.

The closet.—A term applied generally to the managerial department, but sometimes to the "reading closet."

The house.—The general term to express the firm as distinct from anything in connection with the workmen.

Thick leads.—Leads cast four to the pica in thickness are generally thus termed, though thicker leads or clumps are cast.

*Thick spaces.—Spaces cast three to an em of any particular body—the average space used between words.

Thin and middling spaces.—These spaces are cast respectively five and four to an em of their own body, and are kept mixed together in one box in the lower case.

Thin leads.—Leads cast eight to the pica in thickness are generally thus termed, though thinner leads are cast,

*Thin spaces.—Spaces cast five to an em of their own body.

Thirds cards.—A size of card—cut 3 × 1½ inches—used as a " gentleman's " visiting or address card.

Thirty-twomo.—A sheet of paper folded into thirty-two leaves, written shortly thus—32mo.

Thousands.—In casting up the value of composition type is reckoned by thousands—ems in depth and ens in width.

Three-colour machines.—Machines adapted for printing in any three colours.

Three-column.—Matter set in treble columns.

Three-em braces.—Braces cast on three ems of their own body.

Three-em quads.—Quadrats cast to three ems of any particular body.

Three-em spaces. — Spaces—sometimes called " thick spaces "—cast three to an em of any particular body.

*Three-line letters.—Letters used as initials at the commencement of a book or chapter, and let into the text to the depth of three lines.

Three-quarter frame.—A single frame with case rack attached.

Throw in.—A direction to " throw in " or distribute type. Also an instruction to let a page stand into the back margin.

Throw-off impression.—An apparatus attached to a machine for throwing off the impression whilst it is running.

Throw out.—To turn out bad work or work spoilt in printing. Also applied to pages when thrown out into the margin beyond the usual measurement.

Throw up.—An instruction to give prominence to any particular line or lines in displaying.

Throwing in letter.—A synonym for "distributing" type.

Throwing in type.—See "Throwing in letter."

*Throwing quadrats.—Performed with nine em quadrats, which are shaken in the hand and thrown on the imposing surface, the nick side when uppermost only being reckoned.

Thumb lever composing stick.—A composing stick fastened by means of a small lever, instead of the screw with slotted head.

Thumb piece.—The ear or piece of the frisket which is caught in turning up or down the frisket on the hand-press.

Thumb screw composing stick.—A composing stick fastened with a thumb screw, instead of the usual screw with slotted head, and distinct from the "thumb lever."

Tickle's stereo beds.—Large planed iron beds, with slots to allow of catches sliding to any particular part, for mounting stereotype plates.

Tickle's beds.—A shorter term for "Tickle's stereo beds," invented by Mr. Tickle.

*Tie up.—Pages of type when made up are for convenience of handling tied up with page cord and placed on the stone or imposing surface.

*Tight justification.—Matter justified more tightly than necessary.

*Tighten quoins.—To fasten up quoins with the fingers preparatory to locking up, or in hot weather to tighten up quoins to prevent formes falling out.

*Tills.—The cell-like divisions on the top side of the platen of a hand printing press.

Time-work.—Work paid for by a fixed price per hour—distinct from " piece-work."

Tint blocks.—Blocks or surfaces used for printing coloured backgrounds.

Tint surfaces.—See " Tint blocks."

Tinted cards.—Pulp cardboards of various colours—distinct from surface boards.

Tissue paper.—The very thin paper used for interleaving plates in books.

*Title.—The page which describes the work and gives the publisher's name and the date of publication.

Title head.—The blank space at the top of a ruled form or invoice left for the printing of the title.

Title-sheet.—The preliminary sheet of a work, that which contains the title, preface, contents, etc.

Titling letter.—Types used for displaying titles, advertisements, etc.

To make margin.—To make the margins of a forme up to a certain scale.

To make register.—To manipulate the margin so as to ensure perfect register or backing of pages in printing.

To quad out.—To space out with quadrats.

To the bad.—When a workman is in arrear or has been " horsing " work.

To the good.—When anything is to the credit of a workman.

Tobacco papers.—Ordinary paper of set sizes used by tobacconists for holding certain weights of that article.

*Token.—Two hundred and fifty impressions are reckoned as such.

*Token sheet.—A turned-down sheet in a ream of paper indicating " a token."

Tombstone style.—A monumental style of displaying type.

Tommy.—An iron implement for tightening up screws. It has a hole through the head instead of a slot.

Toned paper.—Paper made with a decided tone of different shades—distinct from white or creamy paper.

Top boards.—The upper boards used for laying-on on a printing machine.

Top cover.—The upper or front cover of a book in binding.

Top edges.—The head or top of a book, in contradistinction to fore-edge or tails.

Top gilt.—A description for a book when the top edge only is gilded.

Top side.—The front side of the cover of a book in binding.

Tops.—In stacking work as printed off the warehouseman places a few sheets of each signature on the top, so that they may be at hand if a set of advanced sheets are asked for, thereby obviating the lifting of a quantity of work.

Towgood.—A make of writing paper manufactured by a person of that name.

Town cards.—A size of jobbing card, cut 3 × 2 inches.

Tracing cloth.—A prepared cloth used for tracing purposes.

Tracing paper.—A prepared thin, transparent paper used by draughtsmen for tracing drawings.

Trade customs.—Recognized privileges which have become customary by long usage.

Trafalgar.—A size of type one size larger than Two-line Double Pica and one size smaller than Canon.

Transfer ink.—Special ink for pulling transfers of type or plates for lithographic purposes.

Transfer paper.—Prepared paper for pulling transfers of type or plates for lithographic purposes.

*Transpose.—To shift words, lines, leads, or any portion of matter.

Trans.—An abbreviation of the word "transpose" used in the reading-room.

Trs.—Another abbreviation of the word "transpose."

Travel.—The length or "go" traversed by a machine in printing.

Treadle.—The crank which imparts motion to a machine by means of the foot.

Treadle machine.—Small machines worked by the foot, as distinct from those driven by any other power.

Treble cases.—Special upper cases made to hold three sets of capitals.

Treble-column.—Matter set in three columns.

Trigesimo-secundo.—The bibliographical term for "thirty-twomo," written shortly 32mo.

Trimmed edges.—Edges of books cut or trimmed sufficiently to make them tidy without opening heads or bolts.

Trimmed rollers.—Rollers for machine printing are generally pared at the ends to prevent the composition tearing off the stocks.

Trough.—Receptacles for wetting down paper or for holding lye.

Tub-sized paper.—Paper sized by hand after making—distinct from engine-sized paper.

Tumbler.—A general term for a printing machine with a D-cylinder—one that does not revolve, but reverses in its motion.

Turned commas.—These are used at the commencement of an extract or quoted matter, thus "

Turned out.—If in distributing type a larger number than usual is yielded of any particular sort; or in printing, sheets thrown out.

*Turned sorts.—When a particular letter becomes scarce, another letter is temporarily substituted with its nick reversed.

Turnover apprentices.—Ostensibly apprentices who have been turned over from one firm to another through death or change.

T. O.—These letters are an abbreviation of the word "turn-over."

Turns.—A short term for turned commas or turned sorts.

Turnscrew.—A small flat piece of steel for fastening or un-fastening the screws of composing sticks.

Turpentine.—The spirit used for cleansing ink from wood-cuts, etc., after printing.

Turps.—An abbreviation of the word "turpentine."

Turtle.—A part of the cylinder in a rotary printing machine.

Tuscan.—A fancy open-faced jobbing type.

Tweezers.—Small and finely-pointed nippers used by com-positors for correcting tabular work.

Twelve-to-pica leads.—Leads cast twelve to a pica in thickness.

*Twelvemo.—A sheet of paper folded into twelve leaves, written thus—12mo. Also called "duodecimo."

Twelvemo chases.—Chases with two cross-bars unequally divided.

*Twelves.—A familiar term for "twelvemo."

Twelves points.—Press points made on an elbow.

*Twenty-fourmo.—A sheet folded into twenty-four leaves, written thus—24mo.

Twentymo.—A sheet folded into twenty leaves—written shortly 20mo.

Twicer.—A term of contempt for a man who professes to work both at case and press.

Two-colour machines.—Machines adapted for printing in any two colours at one operation.

*Two-column.—Matter arranged in double columns.

Two-em braces.—Braces cast on two ems of any particular body.

Two-em quads.—Quadrats cast to two ems of any particular body.

Two-feeder machines.—Machines adapted for two distinct layings-on.

Two-line Double Pica.—A size of type one size larger than Two-line Great Primer and one size smaller than Trafalgar—equal to four Small Picas in depth of body.

Two-line Great Primer.—A size of type one size larger than Two-line English and one size smaller than Two-line Double Pica—equal to two Great Primers in depth of body.

*Two-line English.—A size of type one size larger than Two-line Pica and one size smaller than Two-line Great Primer —equal to two lines of English in depth of body.

Two-line Pica.—A size of type one size larger than Double Pica and one size smaller than Two-line English— equal to two Picas in depth of body.

Two-line Small Pica.—A size of type one size larger than Two-line Long Primer and one size smaller than Two-line Pica—equal to Double Pica in depth of body.

Two-line Long Primer.—A size of type one size larger than Two-line Bourgeois and one size smaller than Two-line Small Pica—equal to Paragon in depth of body.

Two-line Bourgeois.—A size of type one size larger than Two-line Brevier and one size smaller than Two-line Long Primer—equal to Great Primer in depth of body.

Two-line Brevier.—A size of type one size larger than Two-line Minion and one size smaller than Two-line Bourgeois —equal to two Breviers in depth of body.

Two-line Minion.—A size of type one size larger than Two-line Emerald and one size smaller than Two-line Brevier —equal to two Minions in depth of body.

Two-line Emerald.—A size of type one size larger than Two-line Nonpareil and one size smaller than Two-line Minion—equal to English in depth of body.

Two-line Nonpareil.—A size of type one size larger than Two-line Ruby and one size smaller than Two-line Emerald —equal to Pica in depth of body

Two-line Ruby.—A size of type one size larger than Two-line Pearl and one size smaller than Two-line Nonpareil— equal to Small Pica in depth of body.

Two-line Pearl.—A size of type one size larger than Two-line Diamond and one size smaller than Two-line Ruby— equal to Long Primer in depth of body.

Two-line Diamond.—A size of type one size smaller than Two-line Pearl and equal to Bourgeois in depth of body.

Two-line English reglet.—Wooden furniture of that depth in body.

Two-line Great Primer reglet.—Wooden furniture of that depth in body.

*****Two-line letters.**—Plain initial letters the depth of two lines, used at the commencement of a chapter or work.

Two-line Pica reglet.—Wooden furniture of that depth in body.

Two on.—To facilitate and economize printing, small jobs are sometimes worked in duplicate.

Two set.—See " Two on."

*****Tympan.**—The frame, usually covered with parchment, on which the sheet is placed in printing at a hand-press.

*****Tympan hooks.**—The thumb-hooks used for tightening the outer and inner tympans together.

*****Tympan sheets.**—The sheets placed between the tympans to soften the impression.

Type.—Stamps cast in metal for printing purposes.

Type bodies.—This refers to the different sizes to which type is cast.

Type cases.—The receptacles in which type is laid for composing.

Type founders.—Firms who cast type; also called letter founders.

Type high.—Anything the height of type.

Type-high chases.—Special chases made the height of type, used for stereotype foundry work.

Type-high clumps.—Metal clumps cast to the height of type, such as are used for stereotype work.

Type holder.—A receptacle for holding type in stamping by hand.

Type lifter.—A slang expression for a compositor.

Type matrix.—A small oblong piece of copper in which a letter is punched which forms the face of a type in casting; also called "strikes."

Type measure.—Scales of wood or ivory used for measuring type.

Type metal.—An alloy specially made for type—differing from stereotype and other metals, which are generally of inferior quality.

Type mould.—The receptacle in which type is cast.

Type music.—Music printed from movable type, as distinct from plate or engraved music.

Type points.—American sizes of types are estimated or calculated by points—Pica being a definite number.

Type punches.—Steel dies which are used for punching a letter into the matrix.

Type scale.—Rules giving the measurement of types of different bodies.

Type slinger.—A slang term for a quick but careless compositor.

Type standards.—The recognized depth in different bodies of type.

Type writer.—A mechanical apparatus for writing by means of type.

Typing.—An amateurish term applied to the setting of any particular line or matter.

Typographer.—A printer from movable types.

Typo.—A short term for typographer.

Typographic.—Relating to the art of printing by means of movable letters.

*Typography.—The art of printing from movable letters.

U

Is the nineteenth signature of the printer's alphabet.

NCUT edges.—Books not cut down, but not necessarily "unopened."

Underhand.—A term used by pressmen in relation to the easy or hard running-in of the carriage under the platen.

*Underlay.—The process of making-ready under type or cuts —as distinct from "overlay."

Under runners.—Continuation of side-notes run under the foot of the page in a similar manner to a foot-note.

Uneven pages.—Pages with odd folios, such as 1, 3, 5, etc.; also called "right-hand" or "recto" pages.

Unfair offices.—This term is applied by society hands generally to those printing offices where the existing scale of prices is not recognized. "Closed" offices are not necessarily "unfair."

Ungathered.—Books delivered to binders in sheets, *i.e.* not gathered into books.

Un-interleave.—To withdraw the sheets which have been placed between printed work to prevent set-off.

Universal joints.—A connection with independent action allowing the free working of any two portions of a machine.

Universal machine.—A jobbing platen machine—for steam or treadle—manufactured by Messrs. Hopkinson and Cope.

Universal.—A short term for the "Universal" printing machine.

Unlead.—To take out the leads from leaded matter.

*Unlock.—To unfasten a forme with mallet and shooting stick.

Unopened edges.—Applied to books the edges of which have not been opened.

Unsized paper.—Paper made entirely without size, and consequently very absorbent and adapted for plate printing.

*Upper case.—The top or upper one of the pair of cases.

Upper case sorts.—Those letters which are contained in the upper one of the pair of cases.

*Upperhand.—Used by pressmen to indicate the movement of the upper part of the press exercised by the bar-handle, the reverse of "underhand," which see.

Upright.—A page or job set or cut to an upright size—the reverse of oblong.

Upright flues.—The main flue or shaft which carries the smoke from the furnace beyond the housetop.

Unsheet.—To withdraw the interleaving sheets between printed work which have been placed there to prevent set-off.

V

Is not used as a signature in the printer's alphabet.

VANTAGE.*—An old synonym for the modern one of "fat."

***Varnish.**—A resinous liquid used very largely in making printing inks.

Vegetable parchment.—Paper chemically prepared to imitate parchment.

Vegetable vellum.—Japanese vellum-paper specially prepared to imitate vellum.

Vellum.—Specially prepared parchment of good quality occasionally used for fine printing.

Vellum laid paper.—A laid writing paper with a vellum surface.

Vellum wove paper.—A wove writing paper with a vellum surface.

Vermilion.—A colour in ink very largely used for rubricating purposes.

Versicle.—A sign thus $\mathcal{V}$ used in prayer books and other religious works.

Vertical engine.—An upright engine, as distinct from a "horizontal" one.

Vesper music.—Plain chant or Gregorian music is thus designated.

Vibrator rollers.—Those rollers on a machine which have a vibrating motion, and convey the ink to the slab for distribution.

Vibrators.—A short term for " vibrator rollers," which see.

Victoria black.—A fancy black-letter character.

Victory machine.—A newspaper machine which prints from the reel, and has cutting and folding appliances attached.

Vigesimo-quarto.—The bibliographical term for " twenty-fourmo," written shortly 24mo.

Vignettes.—A class of illustration with the edges undefined, that is, work tapering or thinning off to the extremities.

Visiting cards.—Cards used by ladies or gentlemen, without an address—distinct from " address cards."

*****Visorum.**—A corruption of the word " divisorium," an article to hold copy on the case.

Vocabularies.—A class of composition taking an extra charge if arranged in columns.

*****Vowels.**—The letters a e i o u and sometimes w and y.

W

Is not used as a signature in the printer's alphabet.

**AFFLE.**—A slang term sometimes used by printers, meaning twaddle, gossip, or "jaw."

Wages bill.—The workman's weekly bill.

Wall box.—A receptacle cut into the wall for fixing shafting.

Walter press.—The printing machine invented by Mr. Walter of "The Times," and used on that newspaper.

Wangle.—A slang term used by printers to express arranging or "faking" matters to one's own satisfaction or convenience.

Warehouse.—The department responsible for printed work and "white" paper.

Warehouse boys.—The lads who assist in the warehouse department.

Warehouse knife.—A large knife used for cutting up by hand small quantities of paper.

Warehouseman.—The workman in charge of the warehouse department in a printing office.

Warped cut.—Woodcuts twisted through dampness, generally caused by improper cleansing or storing.

Washers.—Round flat pieces of metal, used for tightening screws or bolts.

Washing.—An old-fashioned term for "jerrying," or making a noise on an apprentice coming out of his time.

*Washing formes.—Cleaning formes after printing.

Washing up.—The operation of washing up rollers or ink slabs.

Waste.—Surplus sheets of a book beyond the plus copies. Also spoilt sheets used for running up colour on a machine, etc.

Waste cards.—Defective and rejected cards, usually sold at a cheaper rate than perfect ones.

*Waste paper.—Discarded paper from a printing office.

Waste steam.—Spent or exhaust steam.

Watchman.—A little flag of paper placed *pro tem.* in matter as composed, which serves to indicate the position of a footnote.

Watermark.—The wire-mark woven to any particular design in a sheet of paper.

Waver rollers.—Rollers which distribute ink on the ink table in a diagonal direction.

Wavers.—Short term for " waver rollers."

Wavy rule.—Brass rule made with an undulating face, thus ~~~~

*Wayzgoose.—The printer's annual dinner.

*Weak ink.—Poor and thin ink.

Web machines.—Cylindrical printing machines in which the paper is laid on by tapes.

Webbing.—A term for the wider tapes of a printing machine; also applied to the girthing used for running in and out the carriage of hand-presses.

Well.—A receptacle under the cases in the upper part of a composing frame for holding copy, etc.

*Welsh.—The special character of type used for composing works in that language.

Welsh cases.—Cases of special lay for composing works in that language.

Wetter.—The workman whose duty it is to " wet down " paper preparatory to printing.

Wetting boards.—The boards placed between the different reams in the press in the wetting department.

Wetting department.—That part of a printing office where the paper is " wetted down."

Wetting down.—The process of damping paper for printing purposes.

Wetting machines.—Mechanical contrivances for wetting down paper, thus superseding hand wetting.

Wetting trough.—The receptacle for water used in wetting down paper.

Whack !—An exclamation of disbelief much used by printers.

Wharfedale machine.—A cylindrical machine manufactured in Yorkshire and called after the place of that name.

Wharfe.—Short term for the Wharfedale printing machine.

Whatman paper.—A first-class quality of hand-made paper. It can be obtained either laid or wove, and is mostly used for drawing purposes. It is made by Messrs. Balston.

Whatman.—A general term for Whatman paper of any kind.

*Wheel of press.—The drum in a hand printing press round which the girthing winds when running.

Whip.—A slang term for a more than ordinarily quick compositor.

*White.—Any blank space between lines, or the blank portion of a short page is thus termed.

White edges.—Edges of books simply cut—not coloured or gilded.

*White line.—A line of quadrats at the bottom of a page. Also a full blank line of text body when used in a page.

White metal.—Casts in type metal distinct from electrotype faces.

White out.—To space or " branch out " any composed matter, such as displayed or advertisement work.

*White pages.—Blank pages in any portion of a printed sheet.

*White paper.—A general term used for unprinted work— whether white or coloured paper.

White paper register.—To make register without ink by means of impression pulls only.

White paper warehouseman.—In large offices the person responsible for the white paper or unprinted work.

Whitefriars machine.—A newspaper machine of rotary make invented by Mr. Joseph Pardoe.

Whole bound.—Applied to books entirely bound in leather.

Whole fractions.—Fractions cast on one body, thus—$\frac{1}{4}$ $\frac{1}{2}$ $\frac{3}{4}$ —distinct from "split fractions" on half bodies.

Whole frame.—A stand made to hold two pair of cases, with a case rack attached.

*Whole press.—A term used when two men are working at a hand-press.

Wide measures.—Long and wide measures of type, distinct from narrow or short ones.

Wide spacing.—Composed matter which has more than the average space between the words.

*Winter.—The connecting part of the cheeks of the printing hand-press immediately below the carriage or bed.

Wipe.—This is when the rollers catch or deposit an excess of ink on the edge of a forme in printing.

Wipings.—Cotton refuse used for wiping up and cleansing machinery.

Wire mark.—Applied more particularly to those "laid" marks in paper which are seen when the sheet is held up to the light.

Wire sewn.—Books sewn with wire instead of thread.

Wire stabbed.—Pamphlets and similar work stabbed with wire instead of thread.

Wire stitched.—Pamphlets and similar work stitched with wire instead of thread.

*Wood border.—An outside border of wooden rule used for poster and broadside work.

Wood composing stick.—A long composing stick for poster work, made of wood for the sake of lightness.

Wood furniture.—Furniture made of wood—distinct from "metal" or "French" furniture.

Wood letter racks.—Trays placed in racks for holding founts of wood letter.

Wood letter shelves.—Receptacles for founts of wood letter.

Wood pulp boards.—Boards made largely of wood pulp and faced with paper.

Wood rules.—Wooden rules used for the larger class of work, such as posters and broadsides.

Woodcut paper.—A half-plate or rather soft printing paper specially adapted for printing woodcuts and other illustrations.

Woodcuts.—Engravings on wood—generally boxwood.

Wooden press.—The first printing hand-presses were made of wood.

Wool-hole.—An old slang term for the workhouse.

Work and turn.—Half-sheet work on press or machine so imposed as to give two copies on a sheet when printed both sides.

*Worked.—A synonym for "printed."

Worked off.—Any forme or sheet printed off.

Worked-off sheets.—One or two copies of any work laid aside when printed for reference purposes.

Working in pocket.—A term applied to men working in companionships, where each have equal advantages.

Working on lines.—A compositor on piece-work paid by the number of lines composed.

Working on piece.—Workmen paid by the scale of prices in vogue—distinct from "time-work."

Working on time.—Workmen employed and paid by the hour—distinct from "piece-work."

Works.—General term for volume work, as distinct from pamphlets or jobs.

Wove papers.—Papers which do not exhibit wire-marks caused in making—distinct from "laid" papers.

Wrapper.—A thick and strong paper in which reams of paper are wrapped.

Wrapper.—The outside cover, usually of paper, to a pamphlet or similar work.

Wrappered.—A term applied to pamphlets with paper wrappers, as distinct from books bound in cloth or leather.

Wrench.—A tool for tightening screws or bolts on a machine.

Wrinkle.—A fad or notion—a synonym for a "trade recipe."

Writing paper.—Paper of a better and harder nature and more highly sized than that used for printing, adapted for writing purposes.

Writing parchments.—Selected parchments adapted for writing purposes.

Writing vellums.—Fine and selected vellums for writing purposes.

Wrong fount.—Letters of a different character or series mixed with another fount, although perhaps of the same body.

W.F.—These letters stand for "wrong fount."

Wrought iron chases.—Chases made of wrought iron—distinct from "cast iron."

X

Is the twentieth signature of the printer's alphabet.

**YLOGRAPHY.**—Applied generally to the printing of old block-books.

Xylonite.—A chemically prepared substance used occasionally for tint blocks.

Y

Is the twenty-first signature of the printer's alphabet.

**ELLOW edges.**—Books cut and coloured yellow at the edges.

Yellow wove.—A cheap kind of coloured wove paper, but, anomalously, blue in shade.

*Y^c.—The old contraction for "the."

*Y^t.—The old contraction for "that."

Z

Is the twenty-second signature of the printer's alphabet.

 **INC galleys.**—Receptacles on which type is placed, used for slip and newspaper work.

Zinc rules.—Rules cast in zinc—distinct from "brass rules."

Zincography.—The art of producing engravings on zinc by a mechanical process.

Zinco.—A short term for the zincograph process blocks.

Zylonite.—An American method of spelling the word "Xylonite," which see.

www.ingramcontent.com/pod-product-compliance
Ingram Content Group UK Ltd.
Pitfield, Milton Keynes, MK11 3LW, UK
UKHW040832091225
9460UKWH00039B/772